American Non-Fiction

1900-1950

TWENTIETH-CENTURY LITERATURE IN AMERICA

GENERAL EDITORS

WILLIAM VAN O'CONNOR, PH.D.
University of Minnesota

FREDERICK J. HOFFMAN, PH.D.
University of Wisconsin

Fifty Years of American Drama, 1900–1950
by ALAN S. DOWNER, *of Princeton University*

The Modern Novel in America, 1900–1950
by FREDERICK J. HOFFMAN

Achievement in American Poetry, 1900–1950
by LOUISE BOGAN, *poet and critic*

The Short Story in America, 1900–1950
by RAY B. WEST, JR., *of the University of Iowa*

An Age of Criticism, 1900–1950
by WILLIAM VAN O'CONNOR

American Non-Fiction, 1900–1950
by MAY BRODBECK, *of the University of Minnesota*
JAMES GRAY, *of the University of Minnesota*
WALTER METZGER, *of Columbia University*

American Non-Fiction

1900-1950

MAY BRODBECK
University of Minnesota

JAMES GRAY
University of Minnesota

WALTER METZGER
Columbia University

HENRY REGNERY COMPANY

CHICAGO: 1952

Copyright 1952

HENRY REGNERY COMPANY

Chicago 4, Illinois

Manufactured in the United States of America

PREFACE

DESPITE DIFFICULTIES OF DEFINITION, *poetry, fiction, criticism, and drama can be analyzed as literary forms or at least discussed in literary terms. Non-fiction, especially in our time, is another matter. There is a tremendous mass of such writing. Much of it is done with little or no cognizance of the formal patterns of a work of literature. Much of it is ephemeral. But some of it will undoubtedly continue to be meaningful to later generations, perhaps in ways a little or considerably different from its meanings for us. Perhaps only then will it be possible to see with any clarity what these genres or forms were. As contemporaries of such works, we are likely to be more involved with the issues and data discussed in them than with their staying power as literature. And we face the added difficulty that certain genres, the essay and the biography, are not quite what they were for the nineteenth century.*

The nineteenth-century essayist, whether writing in sober earnest or whimsically, was read in good part for his stylistic graces, but the twentieth-century essayist, with few exceptions, has stressed exposition, either in arguing a thesis or in organizing data. We are even a little uneasy with the term "essay" and prefer to use the term "article," partly because the latter term carries no literary connotations. The philosophical essays or articles of a writer like John Dewey, for example, can be read and be widely influential despite their being written in a contorted and obfuscated prose, and occasionally a philosopher has been suspect because *of his stylistic brilliance. It is true, of course, that certain philosophers, economists, and historians have extended their audiences through their craftsmanship and literary style, but these skills have often been looked upon as a grace beyond the essential substance. In other words, influential writers of non-fiction in our time have not always been, in the sense in which the nineteenth century would have understood the phrase, "literary men."*

With American biography the situation is somewhat similar. English biography, thanks to Lytton Strachey, John Maynard Keynes, Virginia Woolf, and a few others, has been more self-consciously an art form. We have had a few able biographers, like Douglas S. Freeman, Carl Sandburg, and Joseph Wood Krutch, but for the most part our biography has tended to be subsumed under history, literary criticism, or even under psychological theory. Again, we have had notable autobiographies, such as The Education of Henry Adams, *undoubtedly a classic, and* The Autobiography of Lincoln Steffens, *more nearly an account of sensational aspects of American city politics than of a man's personal life. With Vincent Sheean's* Personal History *there is, depending upon one's evaluation of it, a reduction of international issues to the journalist's human-interest story or an elevation of human interest to the level of literary expression.*

In other words, our era, at least in the United States, has tended to ignore traditional assumptions about the nature of the literary essay, to merge biography with history, social theory, or literary criticism, and to break down the distinction between literature and journalism. Speculation about the genres or forms which may be evolving within the enormous range of non-fiction would require highly detailed study, much beyond the scope of a brief survey. The editors of this series, therefore, have felt it necessary to have this volume provide not formal literary analyses but general surveys of the works of influential writers of social theory, philosophy (especially as these have been a part of the literary scene or in the consciousness of poets, novelists, or critics), and literary journalism. Each subject inevitably suggests its own appropriate treatment, and it would involve serious distortion to view all non-fiction from the same perspective or to discuss it in the same tone.

Finally, the examination of such a variety and of so large a quantity of writing as has been made by the authors of this book has required a certain amount of condensation. The three essays included here can offer, each in its own way, an extremely useful introduction to their subjects; the Bibliographies will suggest to the interested reader extensions of the treatments contained in the three studies. The editors believe that American Non-Fiction *offers a very good introduction to a class and a body of writing that needs to be acknowledged in any series which proposes to be inclusive in its coverage of materials.*

WILLIAM VAN O'CONNOR
FREDERICK J. HOFFMAN

CONTENTS

American Non-Fiction

PHILOSOPHY IN AMERICA, 1900-1950

MAY BRODBECK

ALL literature," it has been said, "tends to be concerned with the question of reality—I mean quite simply the old opposition between reality and appearance, between what really is and what merely seems." Though the methods and aims of philosophy and literature differ, this is also not at all a bad way to characterize the nature of philosophy. The philosopher wants not only, as does the artist, to exhibit this difference but also to state how, upon reflection, we know one from the other, to articulate the criteria by which we, unreflectively and instinctively, preserve ourselves from gross deception. In another place, the same perceptive critic speaks of "the chronic American belief that there exists an opposition between reality and mind and that one must enlist oneself in the party of reality."[1] To-

[1] Lionel Trilling, *The Liberal Imagination* (New York, Viking, 1950), pp. 207, 10.

gether, these two comments tell the story of a special and fatal conflict of motives, a conflict between the artist's commitment to see life steadily and see it whole and his commitment, in America, to an ideology that locates mind in the realm of appearance and appearance in the realm of the disreputable. Nor were the novelists and critics alone in this inner self-division. American philosophers have shared the implicit metaphysics of their generation. Like the Dreisers and the Parringtons they have been suspicious of mind. But not without provocation. For twentieth-century philosophy in America developed in reaction against a philosophy which held that everything is One and that One is Mind.

i—IDEALISM

Between the genteel tradition of Emerson and Lowell and its anachronistic revival in the form of the New Humanism, academic philosophy in America had its own and, thus far, last engagement with the Eternal. Until about 1900, philosophy in this country was the handmaiden of theology. In the schools the philosophy courses were invariably taught by a clergyman whose function it was to provide a bulwark against heresy in "this day of general and lamentable depravity." During the last quarter of the nineteenth century, men who had been specially trained, usually in Europe, as philosophers rather than as ministers began increasingly to occupy teaching positions in the colleges and universities, but even these men were primarily concerned with problems arising out of the attempt to justify the ways of God to man. They expounded Absolute Idealism, the last, boldest, and most grandiose systematic defense of God, immortality, and eternal values. Christianity had compromised itself into a precarious position by its initial resistance and final capitulation to the onslaught of Darwinism. The old affirmations no longer seemed adequate or relevant, but the old consolations were still needed. There was unquestionably a market for a philosophy which, even if it meant further compromises with Christian orthodoxy, at least would counteract the corrosive influence of mechanistic science by providing a foundation for belief in things of the spirit, in the fundamental intelligibility of the universe, and in the validity of a universal moral code. All this and more absolute idealism not only promised but, after its fashion, delivered.

As ordinarily used, the words "idealist" and "realist" describe a man's character or personality: his attitude toward life. The technical philosophical meanings of these words have only a very tenuous connection with their colloquial usage. In an obvious sense, each of us is shut up within his own mind—my experiences, like my memories, are mine, and yours are yours. Philosophical idealism is the belief that the world stuff is basically mental; "experience," "consciousness," "mind," "will," "idea" are the terms idealists use to characterize the basic substance of the universe. The world, for the idealist, is dependent for its existence on the mind. But Yeats in "Blood and the Moon" has said it better:

And God-appointed Berkeley that proved all things a dream,
That this pragmatical, preposterous pig of a world, its farrow
    that so solid seem,
Must vanish on the instant if the mind but change its theme.

Absolute idealism is an attempt to avoid extreme subjectivism—the belief that the world is dependent upon my knowing it—by postulating an infinite, eternal Absolute Mind or Knower whose idea or thought is the real world. Philosophical realism is the view that the world exists independently of the minds that know it, that knowledge as such makes no difference to the object known. A philosopher may be a realist in the sense just defined and yet be idealistic in his attitude toward life or, conversely, he may be a philosophical idealist in his study and remain a hardheaded realist in his commerce with the world. With this semantical background, let me return to my story.

Absolute or objective idealism was the late nineteenth-century academic revival of transcendentalism, the pre-Civil War American version of German romanticism, the glorification of the inner, spontaneous, clairvoyant impulse as the source of virtue and truth. Partly because its proponents were professional philosophers, notably Josiah Royce of Harvard, and partly because of the intervening influence of the German philosopher Hegel, absolute idealism is much more of a system of philosophy, more highly structured, than was its early romantic predecessor. Yet, their underlying motivations are the same, and they come out in the same place. The precariousness of the human condition seems to imbue man with an overwhelming desire to prove to himself that what he does is the *right* thing to do. The best way to have a moral standard accepted in our society is to prove it, and the best way to prove it is to give it the dignity and stature of fact by showing it to be as universally true and incontrovertible as a law of physics. Another deep-lying need, old as the anguished *warum* of Job, is the desire to know why things happen as they do, why the world is as it is, to find it "intelligible" or meaningful in the way in which a man's behavior is intelligible if we know his purposes. The protest against science by the romantics in Germany, as by Coleridge and Emerson, resulted from the frustration of this need by the scientific world-view. This view of the universe as a meaningless clash of atoms in the void seemed to lead inevitably to what was felt to be a dangerous and de-moralizing ethical relativism. In reaction, the idealists set out to prove the universal necessity of religious and moral truths. In order to accomplish this they elaborated—follow-ing Hegel—a speculative theory of reality which, at one stroke, provided the intelligibility the scientific view lacked and "proved" the universal necessity of moral laws.

For absolute idealism, the Absolute Mind or God is not a creator separate from the world but is the underlying spirit and substance of it. Reality, including individual man, is a completely interrelated organic whole, which is an idea or thought in the mind of God. All minds are held to be es-sentially purposive or directed toward the Good or Abso-lute. God's purpose is to realize himself or come to complete self-consciousness by unfolding his thought in an eternal, in-finite, logical process. Man is one of the finite forms through which the Infinite develops itself. Since man, by virtue of his finiteness, cannot know this whole, his world is imperfect and incomplete. But this imperfection and incompleteness —the evil in the world—is appearance only, since only the whole or Absolute is really real, just as only the whole is truly true. Man's spontaneous self constructs the world of appearance in its attempts to become one with God, to know the Real, by selecting isolated, particular manifestations of the whole. By this process of selection, the Absolute, or Real, or God, appears as the visible processes of history—the spa-tial, temporal cloak of the eternal, unchanging process that is the unfolding of God's mind. The awkwardness of this conception from the point of view of common experience— its contentions that space and time are not really real, being of the world of appearance only, and that the universe is through and through mental—are far outweighed, for some people, by certain gratifying consequences. The Absolute unfolds itself, not capriciously, but according to a plan rationally conceived to fulfill its purposes. Since the goal of the Absolute is the highest good, this deterministic process is a progress, each stage of which represents a higher moral phase. By this teleological conception of the universe evolving according to a predetermined plan, Reality is identified with the Good and an eternal moral order is guaranteed. The ethical sanction is provided by reading off the moral law from the process as it manifests itself to us in the world of appearance—hence, "sermons in stones." Since each stage in the temporal order is a reflection of the infinite Mind, it is necessary and therefore justified: whatever is, is right. In this way, the genteel tradition that preferred to ignore everything but the "smiling aspects of life" was provided with an official philosophy. Moral standards were identified with necessary judgments about Reality. This is wish-fulfillment thinking in the extreme: by injecting ethics into the process, the world is necessarily realizing our ideals for us. It is also a highly sublimated form of narcissism. Idealism expands the ego to include the whole world; the laws of nature become laws of the mind. So we can know everything by pure reason alone.

Despite its inherent absurdity, idealism has frequently struck a responsive chord in the hearts of poets and others concerned with the realm of feeling. In their case it has not been the absolutistic ethical motif that has been the source of the charm. For the modern poet knows well this is a will-o'-the-wisp. Idealism disparages scientific knowledge, what Royce called the "world of description" or appearance, in favor of a higher insight that pierces the veil of experience and views the "world of appreciation" or Reality, the super-sensible realm of values where everything is as it ought to be. This echoes the poet's claim that his knowledge is of a different and higher kind than that of science. Generally, however, the poet insists that he is truer to experience than science, not that he goes beyond it. Also, idealism, both in Emerson and in Royce, was partly an expression of reaction against a crass, industrial world that overvalued getting and spending and the knowledge of things at the expense of that of man and human relationships. Yet the worship of nature, as the reflection of the divine Idea, is but another form of materialism or even scientism. It is, to put it paradoxically, its romantic or idealistic form. This is the weakness of the position. The most compelling appeal of idealism, its strength, lies in the profound psychological truth that, as Milton has Satan say:

> The mind is its own place and in itself
> Can make a Heav'n of Hell, a Hell of Heav'n.

Imbedded in idealism is this wisdom of the race, the insight that from our hopes and fears, expectations and suspicions, we form our own worlds. But to mistake the inner landscape for the outer is madness. The specious plausibility of idealism stems from thus converting a psychological truth into a metaphysical position.

Such was the theme, with minor variations in a minor key, of the most influential philosophy in America at the close of the last century.[2] Yet, despite its grandeur, its ego gratifications, and its edifying effect on the spirit, idealism did not long prevail. It owes its brief reign to the fact that it was a transitional philosophy, between orthodox theism

[2] "Personalism," or personal idealism, was one reaction within the idealistic movement against absolutism's obliteration of finite individuality. Placing greater emphasis on the finite self, it is a form of subjective idealism. But, since it, too, must come to terms with common sense, personalism always surreptitiously slips in an organic whole or absolute. Influential personalists were George H. Howison and Borden Parker Bowne.

and the growing secularism of American thought. It was a compromise, and like all compromises it satisfied nobody. Orthodox Christians naturally opposed the *hubris* of a construction that arrogated to man the authority of the Absolute. The Christian doctrine that God is a person separate from the world which he has created, not merely *thought*, ran counter to the pantheism of idealism. Traditionally, Christianity has been realistic in its philosophy: God's creation is not dependent for its existence on our consciousness, experience, or knowledge of it. Further, the idealistic dissolution of finite selves into the Absolute, their degradation to mere aspects or fragments of appearance having no full substantial existence in their own right, implicitly denied the Christian soul and its personal immortality. Further, this absorption of the individual into the whole, which alone is real, offended not only orthodox religious ideas but was out of harmony with the deeply ingrained American conception of the importance of the individual and the subordinate importance of the whole. The absolutists' deprecation of science as giving, at best, knowledge of the realm of appearance only was a further irritant at this time and place. I need not rehearse the pervasive influence of science. Yet it is possible, if not to overestimate, at least to misjudge the nature of its influence. The Hegelian myth's loss of glamour owed probably as much to a reaffirmation of a still robust sense of reality as it did to the triumph of the machine. If nothing else, the denial that time and space were really real alone required a degree of suspension of disbelief that, whatever may be the case with the Teutonic soul, was more than English-speaking philosophers could long sustain. The revolt against idealism was a movement parallel with the rise of the realistic and naturalistic novel and strictly analogous to the later conflict between the social critics like Parrington, the realistic critics like Edmund Wilson, Malcolm Cowley, R. P. Blackmur, and Van Wyck Brooks on the one hand, and the New Humanists on the other. In each case—literature, criticism, and philosophy—there was an attempt to break away from the genteel tradition that made literature false to life, criticism an excuse for moralizing, and philosophy a branch of apologetics. In philosophy, the break with this tradition took the form of an attack with two fronts, realism and pragmatism. Not until hostilities were over and the common enemy routed, however, did it become clear that the conquering allies had incongruous ideologies, resulting in a cold war whose chill breezes can still be felt along academic halls. But in philosophy as elsewhere, a catalyst was needed to precipitate the reaction against idealism. That catalyst was William James.

ii—WILLIAM JAMES

James defies classification either as a philosopher or as a psychologist. It has been well said that the kind of philosophy a man has depends upon the kind of man he is. This is nowhere more evident than in the case of William James. There is a basic ambivalence in James that is customarily identified as his self-confessed wavering between what he called[3] the tough- and the tender-minded attitudes toward man and the world, between a predilection for a materialistic, fatalistic, pessimistic outlook on life and a more romantic, optimistic one. While this is suggestive and true of James as far as it goes, it fails in a fundamental way to hit the mark. For the unresolved ambivalence in James, and the conflicting elements in his philosophy show that it was un-

[3] "The Present Dilemma in Philosophy," in *Pragmatism* (New York, Longmans, 1907).

resolved, is, in part at least, a reflection of a rather different division in possible approaches to the world. And this division has no necessary connection with tough- and tendermindedness. James was part poet and part philosopher. One half of him wanted to pin down, to catch in all its concreteness, the qualitative richness of life. But he was no less urgently moved by the questions that this experience poses to men of philosophical temperament. Men may certainly be both poets and philosophers, but the attempt to be both at once is bound to fail. Both poet and philosopher start from experience, but the philosopher wants not to reproduce it but to map it, to identify its characteristic features. That is why his talk is full of such abstract terms as quality, substance, law, and concept. He, as it were, puts distance between himself and immediate experience in order to talk about it. The philosopher's words are not the stuff that poetry is made of. If the poetic impulse dominates, the distance that reflection imposes may seem a falsification. Paradoxically enough, philosophies have even been built around this alleged falsification by the intellect. Royce's deprecation of the "world of description" in favor of the "world of appreciation" was such a philosophy. This depreciation of the intellect in favor of what amounts to feeling, though it be called a higher or purer reason, is the fundamental irrationalism of idealism and all its descendants. In other forms it has continued to be influential in philosophy. In Germany irrationalism could show itself nakedly. In America, however, the prestige of science and the climate of opinion being what it is, it could not be unmixed. Thus, we find it in such superficially unlikely and different places as in the philosophies of James, of Alfred North Whitehead, and of Dewey. The influence of Bergson on the first two of these is not without significance. Let us turn then to James and see by what inner divisions he could be godfather to two quite disparate movements in American philosophy.

Belief in free will is the motive that shapes decisively James's intellectual contour. It was, therefore, not the spontaneous, creative self or mind but, rather, the deterministic "block universe" or Absolute of the idealists that provoked his most spirited attacks. Yet, by his vigorous assertion of common-sense realism and his deep commitment to classical empiricism, he provided all the stimulus that was needed by a generation yearning to revolt against the established order of things. Besides mixing the temperaments of poet and philosopher, James had a dual allegiance, to the tough-minded empiricist tradition as well as to the tender-minded religious atmosphere of his father's home. Henry James, Sr., was a Swedenborgian mystic, and his son William always retained a tenderness for religious experience. Intellectually, the mediating link for James was Darwinism. From this combination of commitments and predilections he developed the two aspects of his philosophy, pragmatism and radical empiricism. That these were not dependent upon each other, he himself believed. That they were, in fact, inconsistent with each other, he never saw. And with his abhorrence of system, it is quite possible he would not have been overly disturbed. For he had had a surfeit of system from the idealists. This was, indeed, his first point of attack.

James's essay "The Dilemma of Determinism" (1884) is important, not only because it contains a scathing critique of the romanticist-idealist ethic from the point of view of a man for whom moral things were first things, but because it represents the thin end of the wedge toward his eventual elaboration of the pragmatist theory of truth. The purposive determinism of the idealists, according to which both the good and the evil of the world were but stages in the

unfolding of the Absolute, was intolerable to James. For—
and this was the dilemma—it meant either accepting evil
as an unmitigable necessity or else, seen from the aspect
of eternity, as really good. In either case it made of life a
perpetual moral holiday, without personal responsibility.
Though James was a puritan for whom sin was sin, he was
also of the earth earthy and, moreover, an optimist who believed that evil could, with effort, be banished from the
world. Denial of change was not only false to his sense of
reality, it scandalized his moral sense. The absolutists' unchanging, fatalistic block universe, James felt, denied experience, outraged morality, and blasted hope.

The abstract and the concrete are frequently opposed to
each other, to the praise of one and to the dispraise of the
other, depending upon the temperament of the philosopher.
It will be useful to distinguish between the legitimate, or
true, and the false abstract; between the abstraction that
illuminates and the abstraction that falsifies. To each there
is a corresponding true and false concrete. Illustrations will
multiply. However, one form of the false abstract is that
exemplified in all descriptions of the universe that explain
development in terms of some force propelling things and
individuals along to a goal. This goal may be thought to be
known, as by the absolutists and the Marxists, or unknown,
as in the form of Darwinism held by the literary naturalists, such as Dreiser. The isolation of some force or forces,
whether they be spiritual, material, biological, psychological, economic, or historical, as *the* determining factor in the
course of events, pushing everything and everyone willy-
nilly toward some end of its own is, it should be obvious,
neither good sense nor good science. It is certainly not good
philosophy. It was in reaction against this form of the false
abstract that James insisted that nothing less than a certain

amount of free play in the universe—chance, unpredictability; in short, indeterminism—would justify his faith in the future. This free play he found in the undetermined, uncaused will of man. Just as the recurrent popularity of the view that All is One has been called the "monistic pathos," so there is also the pathos of the indeterminate, the solace which many find in the notion of an essentially ambiguous future. James was more than immune to the charms of the former, but he fell victim to the latter. For he freely admitted that his belief in a free, uncaused will was emotionally and not intellectually grounded. Just as many who, like James, value highly the existence of individuality, the plurality of things and people in the world are mystified by the appeal of the monistic hypothesis, so others, who see hope for the future only in the plans and decisions men make today, are mystified by the attraction of the indeterminate, the emotional appeal of a world left to the mercy of chance. James was aware that he could not prove the existence of chance, aware, too, that its denial underlies all scientific investigation. He was not aware that the denial of chance also underlies all moral responsibility, that guilt attaches to whoever performed the act because the choice was his and his alone, not because it had no causes. But James found the idea of a universe of chance most agreeable. Because he found it so agreeable, because he wished it were true, because, for the same elusive reasons that make some people embrace the One rather than the Many, he thought he would be happier believing it true, he did believe it was true and called upon others to do likewise.

The doctrine James expressed in his essay "The Will to Believe" (1896) is but an explicit statement of the grounds on which he upheld the freedom of the will. In that essay he defended the right to believe the religious hypothesis, "in spite of the fact that our merely logical intellect may not have been coerced." When there are two incompatible propositions between which it is impossible to decide on grounds of ordinary evidence, it is right to believe in the truth of the one which best harmonizes with our wishes and our happiness. Suspension of judgment he considered the last refuge of cowards. One must either believe or disbelieve, and if the evidence is insufficient for rational belief, the reasons of the heart may prevail. The scientist's demurrer, that it was always better to avoid error even at the cost of losing or postponing knowledge, that beliefs based on hopes alone were too highly bought in the long run, James waved away as the protest of a timorous, unadventurous spirit, afraid to incur large risks. The existence or non-existence of God is a matter of intimate concern to men's happiness or peace of soul, but the methods of science cannot help us decide. Its truth or falsity must, therefore, be decided by an appeal to its effects on the individual. If the belief does indeed bring happiness, then it is true. If not, not. James himself found comfort in the notion of a benevolent but limited God who, with the help of man, would see that our highest ideals were fulfilled. So, for him this rather unorthodox Being existed. The curious man-centered nature of this theology is evident. God exists because we believe in him, rather than conversely. But shifting the focus in this way from God to man is characteristic of James. His theism evolved from a concern with man's fate in this world, not from a concern for salvation in afterlife. It is the kind of theism a man essentially naturalistic and humanistic in temper would hold, if he held any, since it shakes the naturalistic boat less than would a categorical assertion of the supernatural, and it makes the very existence of God dependent on the needs of men.

James's pragmatist theory of truth is thus a generalization of the right to believe from religious matters to all matters. It is not, by itself, all of pragmatism. The year 1898 may be said to mark the beginning of the pragmatist movement, for it was at this time, in an address before the Philosophical Union at the University of California, that James introduced the term "pragmatism" into our language.[4] He adopted it, as he states, from his friend Charles Sanders Peirce, a logician and philosopher who taught occasionally at Harvard but who lived for the most part in isolation, outside the academic stream. Peirce made some notable contributions to new developments in logic, but, characteristically, it was another aspect of his thought that caught James's imagination. In 1878, Peirce published an essay called "How to Make Our Ideas Clear" in which he proposed a method for unequivocally determining the meaning of our concepts.[5] The criterion of meaning here formulated asserted that "to attain perfect clearness in our thoughts of an object we need only consider what conceivable effects of a practical kind the object may involve—what sensations we are to expect from it, and what reactions we must prepare. Our conception of these effects, whether immediate or remote, is then for us the whole of our conception of the object, so far as that conception has positive significance at all."

By "effects of a practical kind" Peirce meant the sensible effects or what we would observe if the sentence containing the term were true. This criterion, he felt, ensures a common meaning for terms without which communication among persons is impossible; and it helps settle certain

4 "Philosophical Conceptions and Practical Results" in *Collected Essays and Reviews* (New York, Longmans, 1920).

5 *Collected Papers of Charles Sanders Peirce,* ed. Charles Hartshorne and Paul Weiss (Cambridge, Harvard Univ. Press, 1931), Vol. V, Pars. 388–402.

types of sterile controversy. With a heavy-handed disregard of religious sensibilities, Peirce illustrates his "pragmatic principle" by the wine used in the sacrament. In one interpretation, the wine is a symbol of Christ's blood. In another, the wine is Christ's blood. Is there a difference of opinion? If those who call it blood and those who call it wine both expect the same set of observable—chemical, physical—properties, then, on Peirce's criterion of meaning, both mean the same and not different things. Two sentences have the same meaning if the same observations would verify them as true or false. As James put it, there can be no difference that doesn't make a difference. James further points out that there was nothing startlingly new about this maxim. It was rather an explicit reformulation of the basic principle of British empiricism since the time of Locke and seventeenth-century science. James's recommendation of the maxim as an aid to settling philosophical disputes—is the world one or many? fated or free? material or spiritual?—had already a long history. Bishop Berkeley had stated it almost literally in his destructive analysis of the notion of an underlying, unobservable substance or matter, and Samuel Johnson's refutation of Berkeley by kicking a stone was no refutation at all. Science was long accustomed to using this criterion. As a theory of meaning, then, and subtleties aside, Peirce's pragmatic principle fitted well not only with common sense and science but with a powerful philosophical tradition.

But James was to adapt Peirce's theory of meaning to his own uses. Disarmingly, in that same essay, he suggests that Peirce's principle should be interpreted "more broadly." His emendation of Peirce made capital of the ambiguity in the phrase "practical effects of an idea." Peirce distinguished between the consequences of the object of belief

and the consequences, on the individual, of holding a belief. James did not. Not only the sensations to be expected
should constitute the meaning of an idea but also its "emotional and practical appeals." Thus, since the emotional or
personal effects of believing the sacramental liquid to be
wine or blood may well be different, these are, according to
James's criterion, different ideas and not the same at all. By
including the private practical consequences in the meaning of an idea, James gave Peirce's principle a relativistic,
subjective twist that Peirce did not intend.

Truth, said the idealists, is eternal. And in this most philosophers have concurred: once true, always true. When we
say that an assertion is sometimes true and sometimes false,
this is merely an innocently imprecise manner of speech.
"New York City has more than seven million inhabitants."
True on July 26, 1950; false on July 26, 1917. But, "New
York City had more than seven million inhabitants, on July
26, 1950," if true, is always true, was always true—though
not known before that time—and will always be true. Thus,
it is only a habitual ellipsis of ordinary speech that lends
plausibility to the "sometimes true, sometimes false" assertion. The world changes, but truth does not. Though the
idealists shared this insight, they meant something different
from this everyday, commonsensical eternality of truth. For
Truth, characteristically with a capital T, was for them not
an attribute of statements, expressed by an adjective, but a
thing, expressed by a noun. Truth is Reality. If truth is identified with reality, made a thing or a substantive rather than
an adjective, then there are two alternatives. Admit that reality changes, then truth, too, changes. Deny that reality
changes, then truth, too, is changeless. Neither of these alternatives is very palatable to common sense, but if truth is
a substantive, then this dilemma is inescapable. The ideal-

ists chose the second alternative. In the really real, there is no change, and in it truth resides. In appearance there is change but no truth. Only the whole, the God's-eye view of the universe can be true, for only it is eternal, only it is real.

In James's mind the predetermined block universe, the view that evil is only illusion, the disparagement of the world of experience in favor of a world known by pure reason or intuition, the neglect of the individual in favor of the whole, the denial of change and the belief in immutable truths were all bound together. Thus, he discarded them all together. This was the web of the Absolute, a web in which he would not be caught, making his escape by a path that led from the pathos of the indeterminate over the will to believe to the pragmatist theory of meaning. Add an immersion in Darwinism, a respect for science, and we have the slippery slope that led James to the doctrine that the truth is what works, what guides us in the painful process of adaptation.

"It is useful because it is true or it is true because it is useful. Both these phrases mean exactly the same thing."[6] A belief is to be tested by its consequences for the future. If these consequences will be of value to those who hold the belief, then it is true. James lived in a happier time than ours; so this formula probably did not have quite the cynical, ominous ring to his generation that it has, or should have, to ours. But even in his time men were not saints, and truths, patently, not always useful, nor, just as patently, useful ideas always true. How then explain the vigorous defense of this doctrine on the part of the eminently civilized and urbane James who had nothing but good will in his heart toward his fellow men?

Just as James had played fast and loose with Peirce's cri-

6 "Pragmatism's Conception of Truth" in *Pragmatism.*

terion of meaning, shocking Peirce into a repudiation of "pragmatism" as a name for his own philosophy, so, consistently with that modification, James dallied with the notion of verification. On the one hand, verification meant the public process of dipping into sense percepts; on the other, it meant any consequence that satisfied human needs, had value for concrete life. This vacillation lent specious plausibility to James's insistence that he was speaking straight from the sanctuary of truth, the scientist's laboratory. But even the public process of verification is not the same thing as truth. Ruins and pieces of dust confirm a hypothesis about an ancient civilization, but they are not the same thing as that civilization's full-blooded existence. Observations are said to verify a hypothesis because they are what we would expect if the hypothesis is true. Otherwise, what are they verifications *of*? The concept of verification presupposes the concept of truth. And what if we never had the appropriate experiences, never verified the hypothesis, would it not still be true? The limits of our knowledge surely are not the limits of truth. But truth independent of human experience, needs, or desires was of no interest to James; so, it did not exist.

Out of his intellectual honesty he conceded that if one accepted his definition of truth, then for a certain class of minds even the Absolute must be true, in so far forth as it afforded them comfort and peace of soul. By this "in so far forth" James attempted to retrieve his doctrine from what he considered the "abominable misunderstandings" of the identification of truth with the vulgarly useful, with what pays or has "cash value." Ideas which help rather than hinder, which give comfort rather than pain, are true, but only "in so far forth"—only insofar as they do not clash with other vital benefits, with other beliefs that we must also acknowledge. This is a warning well-taken and well-meant and, in practice, doubtless would limit the number of consoling ideas people cling to for that quality alone. But it is far from an adequate safeguard either in theory or in practice. In practice, one could conceivably cherish a whole consistent system of beliefs that were, alas, false by ordinary standards. Admitting the religious comfort the Absolute gave to some, James nevertheless rejected it for himself because it conflicted, among other things, with his notion of finite responsibility. But if one does not happen to share this sense of personal responsibility, then the Absolute is still, for such a person, true. Theoretically, since, in James's view, it is against all other vital benefits of our own that we must match any single judgment, "in so far forth" does not remove the difficulty that, for the pragmatist, truth is a purely individual affair. The same belief may be true for me and false for you. In point of fact, while James did earnestly try to remove from pragmatism the taint of crassness and cynicism, he wanted at the same time to maintain its relativistic implications. Truth for James, and this is perhaps the heart of the matter, is an ethical concept, a species of good, for it is that which it is *better* for us to believe and, proper utilitarian that he was, it must therefore be admitted to vary with person, time, and place. Conflicts between beliefs are to be resolved in terms of greater moral satisfactoriness.

It is a fact of life that men tend to believe what they like to believe. Pragmatism is the only philosophy that makes a virtue of this human weakness. James's motive, the desire for men's happiness, is far from an ignoble one. But ethical preoccupation must not cloud one's vision of things as they are. And one may, without paradox, insist upon this on ethical grounds alone. It may indeed be the case that if true ideas were not helpful in life's struggles, men would shun truth. Our own time is not without instances. But it is quite another thing to say, as James permitted himself to say, that it would then be our *duty* to do so. James's intuitive feeling for the claims of common sense over fantasy, his strong sense of the absurd and of the potentialities for evil in acquiescence to the absurd, which played so large a role in his battle with absolute idealism, were betrayed by his profound respect for the individual, his tender but misdirected solicitude for the individual's right of choice in his beliefs and in his path of life. Such are the ironies of philosophy.

By his theory of truth James returns full circle to his belief in a universe of chance, for his pragmatism reinforces what he felt to be the happy implications of that view. "Our truths," said James, "are man-made products." And he did not mean this in the trivial sense that when we alter something in the world, a statement that was once false is now true. He meant, instead, that when an individual discovers in his own experience that a certain proposition is true, then that individual has made the proposition true. Our verification makes the idea true. Since truth is made by men, it changes as what men find agreeable or adaptive changes. Thus, James concluded triumphantly, truth is not eternal but mutable. Today's unpleasant truths may be tomorrow's falsehoods; more particularly so if what happens tomorrow does not depend upon what happened *to us* today and yesterday, as it may not if there is the kind of looseness in the world that James conceived. Of course, on the same theory, today's agreeable truths may be tomorrow's falsehoods or, since it is all a matter of chance, the disagreeableness may remain. This is the pathos of the indeterminate. It does not, as James wanted to believe, guarantee the prospect of a better world. Indeed, rationally considered, it makes it less likely, not more so. James's inability to be optimistic and

happy without the belief in chance reflects, I suspect, his
inherited puritan pessimism as to what man could achieve
unaided in the natural course of events. But it reflects also
a certain reluctance to face a hard reality, with its own laws,
to which man must bend, if he is to mold it, as closely as he
may, to his heart's desire. If truth is made by man, the future
is indeed open and limitless in its possibilities. The hard
recalcitrant core recedes into insignificance, and the future
lies, not in the lap of the gods, but solely in human hands.
James's pragmatism is thus, in a human sense, merely a puritanism that has lost its nerve.

James's doctrine that a true idea is one that works, one
that has satisfactory consequences for action, led him naturally to what is known as the "conventionalist" or instrumentalist approach to scientific knowledge: the belief that
such knowledge is merely a tool or instrument for getting
around in the world, a useful convention rather than a revelation of reality. Indeed, this doctrine marks the main direction of the pragmatist impulse in philosophy. James himself
holds it only equivocally. For, partly because his common
sense never fully deserted him, partly because he was concerned with fundamental questions about the nature of reality as well as with human issues, he also implicitly assumed
the converse of his pragmatist statement of truth: namely,
that an idea works because it is true, because in some sense it
reveals or describes the way the world actually is. His radical
empiricism springs from this conviction. It is James's attempt to deal with metaphysical rather than practical problems. In it he presents a description of the nature of reality,
of mind, of the relationship of mind to matter, and of appearance to reality.

The classical British tradition, despite its aggressive empiricism, had not always been entirely true to experience in its description of the world. It tended to pulverize the universe into discrete elements, accounting rather lamely for the experienced relations between these elements, such as the fact that one color is brighter than another and one man taller than the next. James called his empiricism "radical" because it maintained that the relations between elements were as objectively real as the elements themselves. In his graphic language, the flights as well as the perches of experience are "out there." In this surer grasp upon reality James was confirmed by a rather unexpected source, namely, the logicians. For Whitehead and Bertrand Russell in their epochal *Principia Mathematica* (1910) gave primary treatment to the logic of relations, an advance of the greatest philosophical significance over Aristotle who, like the British elementarists, thought only in terms of subjects and predicates, the grammatical reflections of substance and attribute, with relations awkwardly squeezed into that mold. James's insight that, for example, not only the tones but the fact that one tone is higher in pitch than another, that not only the individual tones but the melody, are directly experienced anticipated the work of the European phenomenologists. This insight about relations James applied, in a rather startling way, to the problem of the nature of mind.

Men had always, of course, distinguished between mind and body, between the realm of spirit and the realm of matter. But the rise of physical science in the seventeenth century gave that dichotomy a form which raised problems characteristic of modern philosophy. Physical science then construed and, all details apart, still construes reality as made up of those measurable aspects of experience, called primary qualities, like size, shape, mass, and velocity, upon which all men could agree and among which uniformities or laws can be found to obtain. But human experience consists of a great deal more than this. There are also colors, tastes, odors, and sounds. These, like love and hate, pleasure and pain, are not quantitatively ascertainable, and they vary from man to man. Giving the world its vivid, rich texture, they are nevertheless but "secondary" qualities, effects in us of the primary ones. While the primary was the realm of the physical and real, the secondary, the realm of the mental, was appearance only.

This materialistic picture of the world is the converse of the idealistic one. For both, the greater dignity and value attaches to the real, but while the idealist awards the accolade to mind, the materialist does the honors for matter. James's philosophy of "pure experience" attempts to harmonize his respect for science with his regard for the testimony of human experience.

"Does Consciousness Exist?" asked James in the title of a very influential essay of 1904.[7] No, it does not, was the rather startling answer this former psychologist gave. In his justification of this answer lies James's metaphysics, his view about the nature of ultimate reality. Solicitous as he was for all the vast variety of experience, James did not mean to deny the difference between the mental and the physical, between sensations and things, between dream and reality. He did not mean to deny that in some sense consciousness exists. He denied only that it was a special entity, unique in kind and different from physical objects. The ultimate building blocks of the world, he said, the primal stuff of all things is neither consciousness as for the idealists, nor matter as for the materialists. This neutral stuff which is neither mental nor physical he called "pure experience."

[7] Reprinted in *Essays in Radical Empiricism* (New York, Longmans, 1912).

The phrase was unfortunate, for if experience means anything at all, it means somebody's experience, something that happens to an individual and stands in a characteristic, intimate relation to him. Hence, experience implies a sentient being or mind. It is thus not neutral at all; it is mental, and the whole of James's analysis crumbles because it assumes what it claims to deny. In fact, by the modifier "pure" James meant to deny precisely what experience normally means. A less misleading name for the doctrine that the material from which the world is constructed is neither mind nor matter, but something anterior to both, is "neutral monism." This phrase, by the way, is Bertrand Russell's.

To justify his denial that consciousness or mind is a thing or entity and at the same time to retain the felt distinction between thought and thing, the mental and the physical, James applied his doctrine that the relations between the parts of experience are themselves parts of experience. The same identical terms of pure experience taken in one type of relation constitute the system of external reality, while in another they constitute the stream of thought. Just as the same man in one relation is a father while in another he is a banker, so the same element of pure experience in one relation is mental, in another, physical. Subjectivity and objectivity are, said James, affairs, not of what an experience is intrinsically made of, but of its relations to other things, its context. Experience does not come stamped "inner" or "outer"; these labels are the result of a later classification. Mental and physical fire differ only by the fact that the former won't and the latter will burn sticks. Within pure experience we distinguish between two different sets of relations, the mental context and the physical context. Mental water may or may not put out even a mental fire, while real or physical water always behaves in the same lawful way. In perception, at the point of intersection of the mental and physical orders, there is one and the same neutral element, which is at one and the same time percept and object, idea and thing. Consciousness is one peculiar structure of elements, none of which is intrinsically conscious or mental, while external reality is another such structure, none of which is intrinsically material. Thus, according to James's theory, one may say without paradox that there are minds and there are bodies, but there is no consciousness and there is no matter.[8]

From this theory of reality James derived a distinction between two kinds of knowledge. Direct apprehension, as of the color orange, James called "knowledge-of-acquaintance." In this immediate cognition, mental content and object are identical. But human experience is less than human knowledge. One may never have seen the color orange and yet know that it is the color between red and yellow. This kind of knowledge James called "knowledge-about." The laws by virtue of which we (unconsciously) classify experience as mental or physical are also knowledge-about. For they go beyond immediate givenness, relating it to other kinds of potential experience which we may or may not have. Knowledge-about thus relates the direct sensation to its context, enabling us to classify it as of one kind or another. Knowledge-about also comprehends possible experiences, like the knowledge that there are tigers in India. But all mediate knowledge must be ultimately certifiable by direct or immediate experience. Knowledge-about is consummated by knowledge-of-acquaintance.

James's devotion to the thickness of reality reveals the artist strain, his sensitivity to what has been called the "world's body." To be sure, the idealists also emphasized the con-

8 Presently we shall see how the new realists used this doctrine.

crete and immediate; but there is a significant difference. For them, this unique, sensuous experience was ineffable, inexpressible in words, to be appreciated but not described, for one is speechless before it. For the absolute idealist, only the whole or context is real; the fragments, the qualities isolated from their relations are nothing. To the sheerly qualitative we can merely respond emotively and inarticulately. James agreed that our feelings and sensations do not come named and are, in this sense, dumb. But as we proceed, by knowledge-about, to the context and identify our percept as one of a kind, then we can name it; it is no longer speechless, and the name denotes a reality. The thickness, concreteness, and individuality of experience, complemented by and complementing the conceptual is, for James, what in the end our knowledge is about and what our language expresses. Knowledge-by-acquaintance is knowledge of the world's body.

James's resolution of the dualism between mind and body by use of the indisputable fact that a thing may, without contradiction, belong to two classes at one and the same time has been frequently criticized, not without justice, as somewhat overingenuous. Still, his radical empiricism offers us a suggestive analysis of the nature of knowledge and reality and is, as far as it goes, consonant with both science and art. This is no small merit. Moreover, his insistence that all knowledge-about must end in knowledge-of-acquaintance redresses the more absurd implications of his pragmatic theory of truth. Yet, the anti-intellectual tendencies of his will to believe and his pragmatism, with their stress on emotion and practicality, were to reassert themselves in his later philosophy when his contact with the work of a very popular French philosopher encouraged him to adopt, during the last years of his life, a rather different form of irrationalism.

With his customary graciousness, in a 1909 essay, James acknowledges the influence of Henri Bergson.[9]

Happily, it is not necessary for our purposes to attend to the details of Bergson's philosophy. With much of it James could not possibly agree, for it is essentially another variant of idealistic, Hegelian monism. It is saved, however, from the block-universe implications of absolute idealism by grace of the *élan vital,* which, like Schopenhauer's cosmic Will aiming at self-realization, is the cosmic force in and by which all individuals live and move and have their being. Still, by casually and carelessly identifying his own pluralistic pure experience with Bergson's absolute intuition, in which all plurality is dissolved into a unity that passes understanding, James found in Bergson much to suit his taste.

For Bergson, mind is more than suspicious; it has been tried and found guilty. The intellect, he believes, necessarily misrepresents and falsifies in the interests of practice. Our only access to reality is, therefore, through instinct or intuition. Like Bergson, James came to believe that concepts are only tools that cannot yield real insight since they fail to connect us with the inner life of the flux.

Both Bergson and James were temperamentally attracted to the living pulse of things, experience at its most intense and vivid. The root evil of all discursive knowledge they therefore found in its being analytical. The cuts or abstractions analysis makes into experience are expressed by concepts which are static, while life itself is ever changing. This is why analysis necessarily falsifies the living pulse of things. The absolutists had argued from the immutability of concepts to the immutability of the world. This, James expostulated, was absurd. But James accepts the premises of the

---

9 "The Compounding of Consciousness" and "Bergson and Intellectualism," both in *A Pluralistic Universe* (New York, Longmans, 1909).

enemy when he rejects concepts because they are not replicas of experience. A concept is true of an entity if it applies to some aspect of it, not if it shares that aspect. Our concept of life doesn't live, and growth doesn't grow. Experienced duration is, to be sure, radically different from the concept of motion as change of place with respect to time. Nevertheless, experience is not falsified when its elements are disclosed. Everything is in flux, but within that flux there is constancy of pattern. This pattern is what science calls laws. Though one flash of lightning is indeed different from every other, a unique event, and one crash of thunder is similarly unique, still amongst all the change and uniqueness, there is something changeless: namely, the qualities of being thunder and being lightning and, also, that their instances always follow each other. Science is merely the modern form of the old search for the eternal and the unchanging. Only, unlike idealism, it finds its constancy not in some realm beyond change but within the realm of change itself. James's distrust of concepts, in which he was encouraged by Bergson, is thus without foundation.

James's concern for the concreteness and uniqueness of each particular of the world had most felicitous consequences in his social philosophy. The metaphysical consequences were less happy. He was, in the end, led to the ineffable. For to use language at all is to use concepts. One cannot speak of the greenness of green things or the wetness of individual raindrops without using concepts. Language thus reflects another aspect of the constancy in the world. One raindrop may be unique and much different from another, as one sunset may differ from another, but there is something about them that is the same, by virtue of which we call them both raindrops or both sunsets. Each moment is fresh, but its content is not wholly so. This sameness in succeeding moments of time and in all the separate things of the world we express by concepts. By means of them we describe the world about us, describe even its rich variegated quality, describe the way in which one experience differs from another. The more concepts we have at our command, the more nuances of feeling or sensation we can communicate.

If it is not realized that novelty and uniqueness are merely the novelty or uniqueness of patterns consisting of characters that may have many instances, then language fails. Experience can neither be communicated nor reflected upon; it can only be "lived," where to live means to absorb oneself into sympathetic, mystic communion with the thickness of things. The specious cult of uniqueness has had its devotees in literature, too. According to them, each poem is a concrete, unique particular. It may be unique, but it is not, in a philosophical sense, a particular. If its words were not general, or concepts, if the poem did not share something with other communications, it would be utterly incomprehensible. Criticism, in turn, would dissolve into aesthetic impressionism. Anything wholly unique is inexpressible.

To every false abstract there is the corresponding false concrete. It is false to assume that for every general term there is an entity it names. There is no state over and above the individuals and institutions that make it up, no university over and above its several components and the way in which they are related. But the concreteness of the ineffable is equally false. Yet James believes that Bergson "is absolutely right in contending that the whole life of activity and change is inwardly impenetrable to conceptual treatment and that it opens itself only to sympathetic apprehension at the hands of immediate feeling."[10] He does not see that

10 *A Pluralistic Universe,* p. 342.

such irrationalism makes even knowledge-of-acquaintance forever dumb. If the experienced quality cannot be named, since naming classifies it as one of a kind and it is real only in its ineffable uniqueness, then we cannot speak. And if we cannot speak, there is no philosophy and, for that matter, no literature.

There was another, not unrelated, aspect of Bergson's philosophy which James found congenial. This was the doctrine of "creative evolution." Since each moment is wholly unique and there is no constancy, not even in the way things change, since nothing ever repeats itself, so that no two things are in any aspect alike, the world is ever in the making. It is not made and changing—change implying change of something that already was—but being created, producing itself as it goes along. Each stage in the evolution of life is not, as in Darwinism, due to a combination of elements that existed beforehand and are now brought into a new pattern, such as a new species. Each stage brings with it something altogether new. New qualities may appear which are in some sense conditioned by the past but which cannot be inferred from it. This novelty emerging in time through the purposeless activity of the vital force is thus wholly unpredictable. Or, to say the same thing differently, such a world would be radically indeterministic. Thus we come full circle in the philosophy of William James.

From Bergson and James we turn quite naturally to the philosophy of Alfred North Whitehead, for the three have much in common.

iii—ALFRED NORTH WHITEHEAD

Alfred North Whitehead, an eminent mathematician and co-author with Bertrand Russell of *Principia Mathematica*, was an Englishman who came to this country as a Harvard professor in 1924 at the age of sixty-three and stayed until his death in 1947. Since he turned to philosophy only in his later years, most of his philosophical work was published after he had come to America. Whitehead's writings, difficult to understand, abound in new words for old ideas as well as in old words that are used in a new sense, a practice not conducive to clarity. The great popularity of *Science and the Modern World,* which is hardly a "popular" book, is probably due to the appeal of certain views Whitehead expresses there in a few less technical chapters. One cannot be sure that one understands his philosophy in all its ramifications. Some of its major outlines, though, are relatively clear.

In *Science and the Modern World* (1925), Whitehead pays special tribute to both James and Bergson: to James for inaugurating a new stage in philosophy; to Bergson for being the philosopher most characteristic of the epoch. By denying that consciousness was a unique stuff or entity, James is held to have remedied that seventeenth-century "bifurcation of nature" into matter and mind, with its correlative division of primary and secondary qualities, by which, according to Whitehead, "modern philosophy has been ruined." Bergson, he thinks, is representative because he proclaimed, in the name of philosophy, an organic theory of nature. Unless this is done, Whitehead says in that same work, the poets comprehend the concreteness of this world more adequately than do the scientists. For the scientists' bifurcation of nature makes the fullness of concrete experience, which is the artists' world, unreal. Whitehead's philosophy, like James's, is one great protest against materialism, against the denial of reality to sense qualities, against scientific determinism and its "mechanical" explanations. His solution is a "philosophy of organism and organic mechanism." In some ways Whitehead is thus not unlike the Bergsonian James. In others, he is radically different.

Whitehead has no use for the "billiard-ball" conception of a world made up of hard little particles endowed with only primary qualities and ruled by Newton's law of attraction. In this scheme of things, nature becomes a "dull affair, soundless, scentless, colourless; merely the hurrying of material, endlessly, meaninglessly." Though this Newtonian "world machine" was enormously successful, all of modern science having been built on it, it is yet, says Whitehead, a most incredible conception. He explains the paradox of its success, as do James and Bergson, by his analysis of abstractions or scientific concepts. He agrees with Bergson that scientific concepts distort nature; he denies that this distortion is the price one must pay for intellectual comprehension. Rather, the error is accidental—the mistaking of the abstract for the concrete. It is, in his famous phrase, the fallacy of misplaced concreteness. To avoid it, one has merely to return to concreteness, to the "immediate facts of our psychological experience."

The point is best explained by an illustration the physicist Eddington once gave for the method of science. Suppose that a purple elephant is sliding down a green, grassy hill. To discover the time of descent the scientist abstracts from this charming situation the mass of the elephant, the angle of inclination of the hill, and the coefficient of friction. Nothing else. The elephant, the hillside, the softly yielding turf, the colors all fade out of the picture, for they are not relevant to the solution of the problem. With them the poetry, the charm, the sensuous reality have faded, too. The distortion is thus also a simplification. It simplifies by neglecting individual distinctions; by taking account of only those elements of a situation that are relevant to a particular problem; or, more generally, by formulating laws, that is, those aspects of experience which uniformly recur. Laws do not relate concrete situations but abstractions, or slices, from these situations. But unlike Bergson and James, Whitehead does not deny reality to the scientist's concepts. These concepts are not unreal because they are abstract. They are abstract because, unlike sense concepts, such as the names of colors and textures, they do not name what is immediately given. Whitehead admits that abstract entities are part of the furniture of the world and, being this, produce the successes of science, such as they are. Yet they do not pursue the unique, that which, as Whitehead puts it, has a "simple location," is an "event" with a definite position in a definite region of space throughout a definite duration of time. The unique, he feels, can only be arrived at by indirect construction from the concrete reality. Even our immediate concrete experience is not unique but eternal and repetitive in that we directly apprehend instances of sense concepts. For even these concepts, such as redness and circularity, since they are concepts, are universals or, in a Platonizing phrase, "eternal objects." They are abstract in that they transcend particular concrete occasions of actual happening, that is, particular red patches or circles. So Whitehead's case against science in this instance reduces not to an attack against the use of abstraction as such, as in Bergson and James, but to an attack against all but qualitative abstractions. But if this were all Whitehead objected to he might have erected a philosophy much like that of one branch of logical empiricism which, as we shall presently see, holds that scientific concepts are all ultimately definable in terms of the directly experienced, or, in James's terms, that all knowledge-about is grounded in knowledge-of-acquaintance. But Whitehead found much more in the directly apprehended than mere sense concepts such as colors, tastes, odors, textures, and sounds. Here, also, is the root of his sympathy for and affinity with Bergson.

Whitehead protested not only against what he considered the materialism of seventeenth-century science, the leaving-out of the felt richness of reality as it impinges upon us, but also against its use of mechanical explanation, the view that "the molecules blindly run," as Whitehead himself, adapting Wordsworth, once put it. The scientist does not seek explanation in terms of purposes but only in terms of causes. Nor does he find any inherent connection between cause and effect, some power in the cause by virtue of which it brings forth the effect. Cause and effect are, for the scientist, merely names for two kinds of events that observation finds to be uniformly, invariably correlated. The scientist rejects, as primitive animistic thinking, the popular tendency to attribute to causes something analogous to human effort, something like muscular tension or the feelings of activity and passivity in us when we either push or pull. Regularity of sequence, with no reference to purposes or motives, is the essence of mechanical explanation, whether it be of that branch of physics known as mechanics, or of electrical phenomena, or of organic behavior. The term "mechanical," as applied to all non-purposive explanation, is only a historical carry-over from the time when mechanics was the first and virtually the only successful science. Whitehead's objections to mechanical explanation are therefore broader than his strictures against materialism, directed as they are against everything that is generally known as scientific explanation. And Whitehead has indeed the courage of his convictions.

He contends that our concrete experience belies a scientific view that has no room for vital connection between events and for some ultimate purpose guiding all processes. What Wordsworth found in nature but failed to find in science was not only the felt quality of things in themselves but a sense of the togetherness of things, of a unity pervading separateness, of a connection between events as vital and immediate as that between our wills and our acts. This felt relatedness and direction of things must, says Whitehead, be recaptured in our philosophy. Of course, others before him had reacted against scientific explanation in the realm of living substance. This reaction was expressed in the doctrine of "vitalism," so popular with Samuel Butler and George Bernard Shaw. Vitalism accepts a purposeless, mechanistic explanation on the level of the inanimate but holds that on the level of living matter something new appears or emerges, something that acts as the directive force, so the molecules do not blindly run. Whitehead, however, explicitly rejects vitalism, not because it does not do justice to the living organism, but because it is not organic enough, because it too accepts a bifurcation of nature, a break in its continuity. Organism, in other words, is everywhere and everything. Whitehead's theory of organism views all phases of existence as of the kind manifested in human life, differing only in degrees of complexity. Everything, down to electrons and protons, has characteristics which we ordinarily think of as exhibited only within human experience.

The logic of all this is straightforward and simple enough. If we are to avoid bifurcation, we must consider everything as behaving in a purposive manner. Every event is an activity, an urge after greater fullness of being. The iron filings leap to a magnet in order to further their own activity, as a human being chooses food to sustain life. Everything responds to or shows feelings toward something else. This process Whitehead calls "prehension." The universe is a system of such prehensions and their interaction with each other. Every entity is itself an organism to be understood only in terms of its relations within the whole, a more inclusive organism. This is the theory of organic mechanism. Each individual life history, each grain of sand, each cell in the body is what it is by virtue of its place in a larger life history, changing its nature as that larger pattern changes. Nor is this change purposeless or unprogressive, as in the mechanical theory of evolution; it is the expression of an underlying activity. And this activity is not, like Bergson's *élan vital*, a blind force creating a world without order, a world driven along by sheer impulse. It is creative and is the ultimate source of all creativity, of new concrete patterns in the world. This source, mediator between the dualism of actual happenings and the eternal objects they exemplify, Whitehead calls God. While God is himself the ultimate irrationality, since no reason can be given for his nature, he is also the last ground of all rationality or order in the universe. The organic connections among individual entities are guaranteed by God's "feeling" their togetherness. Novelty occurs when God's feelings actualize eternal objects not yet exemplified.

Whitehead's organic mechanism, his analogical extension to the inanimate of categories generally thought appropriate to life only, his stress on the interrelatedness of all things, his need for an embracing purpose, all make his philosophy seem to echo nineteenth-century idealism. There are, however, some significant differences. Whitehead does not view concrete actuality as mere appearance of the eternal. For him, actuality, eternal objects in their concrete exemplification, is *the* value in the world. The becoming actual of an eternal object is the presence of more value in human life.

Though God's "feeling" is responsible for the actual world in a way reminiscent of the consciousness of the Absolute, God is not, for Whitehead, responsible for all events. Whitehead's God is finite, not infinite. Nor is the human being identified with God; his acts are, therefore, his alone, though God suffers or enjoys them. In this way Whitehead absolves God of responsibility for evil in the world.

iv—JOHN DEWEY

John Dewey is, of course, more than a philosopher. He is an American institution. Not only philosophy, but social, political, and legal theory and practice, historical method, literary criticism, our whole climate of moral opinion, and, especially, educational doctrine have all felt the impact of instrumentalism, as Dewey calls his variety of pragmatism. For better or for worse, this is an impressive achievement; certainly it requires examination.

Dewey's philosophy moves, as it were, on two levels. On one, it consists of certain attitudes toward man, nature, and society. It insists that man and all his works are part of the natural order, accessible to study just like anything else, with no need of appealing to any extra- or supernatural realm either for the sake of explanation or for the sake of salvation of man and his world. In this, instrumentalism is naturalistic. It is humanistic in its belief that man is the measure of all things, that good and evil relate to actual interests and desires of men. It is melioristic in its ardent advocacy of social reform. Temperamentally, despite significant differences, instrumentalism is, among other things, also the heir of the eighteenth century. Like the men of the great Enlightenment, instrumentalists take a healthy-minded view of man and his fate. To adapt Howells's famous phrase, they see the smiling aspects of human nature. They also share the Enlightenment's confidence that man can, by applying his intelligence, make life on this earth, which is the only earth we have, worth living. Politically, instrumentalism is liberal democratic, insisting as it does that the good society can be built only by the spontaneous, active participation of all. To a very large number of Americans today much of this is almost painfully trite. And a great number of Dewey's writings do seem to be laboring the commonplace. Yet, in fairness it should be pointed out that Dewey, born in 1859, the year in which the *Origin of Species* appeared, lived his young manhood when these things were not all taken for granted. That they are today is in large measure due to the efforts of Dewey and of the generation he soon came to lead. Just how much of this optimistic creed may be taken for granted is another story about which I shall have to say something later on. But beneath this broad creed, this *Weltanschauung,* there is a second, deeper level to Dewey's philosophy. For he had elaborated at length technical or, at least, would-be technical theories of truth, of value, and of reality. And these theories were all very important as the theoretical vehicle of his influence.

For the eighteenth century, Newton was the hero, physics, the model science. For the nineteenth century, Darwin was the bringer of light, biology, the paradigm. If this be possible, Dewey was even more under the Darwinian spell than was James. The biological categories of process, development, continuity, change, and novelty dominate his thought, are ubiquitous in his writings. The genetic method, the explanation of things in terms of origin and function, is for Dewey the only fruitful and legitimate one in answer to all questions in all fields. Like so many nineteenth-century philosophers, Dewey was a philosopher-psychologist and had,

in 1886, published the first American textbook in psychology, an exposition of the then new experimental introspec-
tionism and of physiological psychology, original only in
being strongly flavored with the metaphysics of absolute
idealism. For, unlike James, Dewey's first allegiance in philosophy had been to the Hegelian tradition. Only after he
had come under the influence of James's famous *The Principles of Psychology* (1890) and of evolutionary theory did
Dewey and the gathering crowd of his followers begin that
great attack against idealism, of which they were to form
one major prong. In this attack Dewey found also the scope
he sought for his melioristic principles. Dewey's dissatisfaction with Hegelianism was of a special kind. What he dis-
liked in absolute idealism was, so to speak, the absolutism
rather than the idealism. Deeply impressed by the achieve-
ments of science, concerned above all else with a better life
in this world, Dewey preferred to place his trust in the natural evolutionary processes rather than in the supernatural
dialectic of ideas. Furthermore, the rigidly deterministic
unfolding of the Absolute was repugnant to Dewey, as it
had been to James, since it restricted the freedom of creative intelligence to affect the direction of the process.

Mind, according to Dewey—and, for that matter, according to anybody else as long as we speak as scientists—arose
in the process of man's adjustment to his environment. It
is called into play in order to satisfy some felt need or to
solve some practical problem, and it is judged by how satis-
factorily it fulfills this function. For Dewey, this original
function of mind remains its only function. Purely intellectual knowledge of reality is static, is not really knowledge. Real knowledge is, by its very nature, practical, not
contemplative, a means to action. Not surprisingly, then,
an idea is true, or, in Dewey's phrase, for he shuns even

the word, an idea has "warranted assertibility" insofar as it is a tool useful for some purpose. Ideas are not statements about reality but plans of action and, therefore, like any other stratagem, should be judged by their success in doing what they are devised to do. I have already had my say about James's criteria of use and satisfaction. What was said then applies, of course, equally to Dewey. Only, Dewey gives these criteria a social emphasis not to be found in James.

For Dewey, the idea is to be judged in the light of all interests it affects, those of the person that entertains it as well as those of other persons and groups. Warranted assertibility is, so to speak, truth by Gallup Poll. But this, we are assured, is the proper conception of truth in a democracy. This most dubious feature of instrumentalism, the tendency to impute political or moral characteristics to theoretical issues for which they are not relevant, undoubtedly accounts for much of its popularity. It also accounts for the popularity of Marxism with other people in other climes. And are not instrumentalism and Marxism genetically akin in that they both descend from Hegelianism? Be that as it may, most men being interested in the practical consequences of ideas, a philosophy that holds such dangerously pragmatic views is almost bound to be popular with the many. Instrumentalism articulates this pseudodemocratic prejudice of its culture, of our culture.

The tremendous contribution science has made to man's control of and adaptation to his environment exhausts, for Dewey, its whole nature, is its whole and only justification. Unlike other philosophers, Dewey does not, except in the most vague and cavalier fashion or, even worse, in sociological categories, discuss the nature and limits of scientific knowledge. I said even worse because this is, patently, not a sociological matter. Yet Dewey reveres science, almost as an article of faith, for its practical utility and, especially, for the possibilities it opens to social engineering. As a consequence of this preoccupation with the biological and social origins and uses of science, scientific method or "intelligence" has become the battle cry of the countless disciples who have little or no understanding of what the scientific method is or why it is indeed so successful. Hence, the simple-minded equation between science and democracy; hence, the shallow conviction that there are no questions, social, moral, aesthetic, or philosophical, which science cannot and, in the long run, will not answer. But one must, in Dewey's case as in all others, make allowances for the place and the time. There was doubtless a period, around the turn of the century, before the social sciences were as flourishing and the social scientists as powerful as they are today, when to fight for the extension of scientific method to all realms so that it may do what it can do (which, indeed, is not little) was to fight the good fight. Dewey has never seemed to realize that the battle has long since been won. As always, the revolutionaries of yesterday are the stalwarts of today. But again, in his case as in others, this is not entirely due to everyone's remaining fixed in the battles of his most active period. It also has deeper roots in the whole of Dewey's philosophy.

Zola, in enunciating his program for the naturalistic novel, asserted: "The metaphysical man is dead; our whole territory is transformed by the advent of the physiological man. . . . study men as simple elements and note the reactions. . . . what matters most to me is to be purely naturalistic, purely physiological." If "physiological" is replaced by "practical," this pronouncement expresses very well Dewey's attitude toward philosophy. But, as Bertrand Russell once said, "contempt for philosophy, if developed to the point at which it becomes systematic, is itself a philosophy; it is the philosophy which, in America, is called instrumentalism." Dewey's hostility toward philosophy makes him dismiss all the traditional philosophical problems. The rejection is justified philosophically by three rather different arguments. The first rests on his belief that any question not raised in science is not worth asking. And the scientist, either physicist or psychologist, does not, as a scientist, ask philosophical questions. He takes for granted the common-sense view that our world is a real world, that other people and physical objects existing in it can be investigated by empirical methods, that knowledge is not a puzzle but a natural fact like digestion or love, that the individual and his environment are merely different parts of a whole or system, that the human organism is a psychophysical unit of which the mental and physical are merely different aspects. It follows that, *as far as science is concerned,* the traditional dualisms between mind and body, man and nature, subject and object are merely artificial abstractions or even vicious ones if they tend, as has happened historically, to restrict the permissible range of empirical investigation. And philosophical paradoxes that arise if one begins to question the articles of this animal faith are indeed no concern of the scientists. Nor do they concern Dewey.

When it has once been pointed out that knowing is, after all, a natural process carried on by a certain class of organisms, then the whole so-called problem of knowledge has been disposed of. This is the instrumentalist's theory of knowledge. And, in this sense, instrumentalism hardly has a theory of knowledge. But this adoption of the working scientist's perspective in lieu of an epistemology underlies only one of the three arguments for the dismissal of all traditional philosophy.

Another is sparked by Dewey's intense and, alas, intensely

American indignation against those who deliberately choose the contemplative life, who do not believe that the only justification of either knowledge or wisdom or sensibility or even of goodness lies in their practical consequences, in some very crudely conceived bettering of human existence. Traditional philosophy or metaphysics, it has been said, bakes no bread. Dewey cannot forgive it this "unproductivity," any more than William James could forgive his brother for his novels. Or, to be more scholastic and, at least in this sense, more philosophical, since on the genetic account understanding is not the mind's original function, it cannot now be a valid function. The needed "reconstruction of philosophy" must, therefore, turn away from everything that is pure in the sense in which some believe that there is pure knowledge; and it must face the great social and moral defects and troubles that beset contemporary humanity. Philosophy reconstructed will assume a practical nature, will concentrate upon clearing up the causes of conflict in the world, will become a tool for dealing with these evils. In short, philosophy and philosophers must devote themselves to social engineering. Whoever cares for the old intellectual problems which are, admittedly, of no direct practical consequence is castigated with frank "malice prepense"[11] as a political reactionary, as the kept supporter of a privileged leisure class. The imputation of evil motives to the most disparate of noninstrumentalist philosophers takes the place of a logical refutation, on their own merits, of the views held by these philosophers. The similarity to Marxism is obvious. But again, it is only fair to point out that Dewey is in all this much more restrained, much subtler, and much more dignified than his disciples, just as Parrington is not quite as blind

11 *Reconstruction in Philosophy* (New York, Holt, 1920, p. 24; Mentor Book edition, p. 44). This book contains, in summary form, virtually all of Dewey's views.

as the latter-day sociological critics, Marxist or otherwise. For Dewey is, after all, not only a man of influence but also, in his single-minded absorption in his own thought, a man of stature. There is, as I said, a third ground on which instrumentalism discards all previous philosophies. This ground is, as I use the term, itself metaphysical. For it is Dewey's theory of reality. But then, such is the structure of the system that the shortest path to an understanding of Dewey's ontology leads through a study of his ethics. Of course, this being so is in itself most revealing.

Dewey himself often said that the motive behind his philosophy was his desire to heal the breach between "something called 'science' on the one hand and something called 'morals' on the other."[12] This dualism disappears, Dewey contends, once it is recognized that the scientific method is just as applicable to morality as it is to nature, that by means of it one may determine not only what is but also what ought to be. Standards, just like ordinary scientific hypotheses, may be empirically verified in action. (One recognizes the echo of James's utility!) When Dewey asserts that one can empirically test statements about values, he does not, therefore, merely mean that one can thus test statements about the occurrence of valuations among individuals and cultures, which is uncontroversial and is the sort of thing psychologists and anthropologists actually do or, at least, try to do. For such occurrences are indeed facts like all others, and no dispute should exist about their being open to scientific investigation. Theoretical philosophy or metaphysics explores the logical nature of value judgments and the ontological status of the experiences they describe. Morality, practical philosophy, or, if you please, philosophy in the

12 "From Absolutism to Experimentalism," *Contemporary American Philosophy*, Vol. II (New York, Macmillan, 1930), 23.

broad sense in which the philosophical life is the examined life, appraises the values men do hold. Incidentally, all great theoretical philosophers have always been also concerned with this critique of morals and, Dewey to the contrary notwithstanding, not always in the interest of special privilege or the leisure class. The novelty is Dewey's belief that evaluations are themselves subject to scientific test since they are not different in kind from, say, statements within physics. It is not too much to say that the whole structure of instrumentalism is determined by Dewey's conviction that this continuity between science and morals can be established and, in the interest of the good life, must be established. Instrumentalism, like absolute idealism, anchors the good in the world. In this there is no difference. The difference is that the world, the real, is not the Absolute but, as we shall see, the evolutionary process. And that, of course, is also the way in which Dewey's ethics and his theoretical view of the nature of reality are predicated upon each other.

Dewey vehemently denies that there are any ultimate or final ends or standards that universally and unconditionally oblige all men at all times and all places, regardless of their actual desires. This, forever reiterated, leads many to consider and reject pragmatism as just another variety of ethical relativism. Yet the similarity is superficial. One of the most formidable arguments in the arsenal of relativism is to the effect that one cannot, without accepting either religious revelation or a special moral intuition, single out any particular ethical system as the true one. Dewey rejects revelation and rejects intuition, whatever that is, either moral or otherwise. But he also believes that a scientific morality—and that is, let there be no mistake, the true morality—is possible. Whatever the intellectual case for relativism, and, in a secular scientific frame of reference, it is a very strong one, it is no doubt hard to live up to. Indeed, it is this difficulty which gives color to the argument of those absolutists who claim factitiously that relativism *implies,* logically or at least causally, first licence and, eventually, decay. For, as I have pointed out before, men's need to prove their values is strong. So we need not impugn the absolutist by attributing to him the desire to impose his own values on everybody else; and we may admit that there is something to his fear that unless our moral standards have some kind of objective validity, moral chaos cannot be staved off. The hard fact that the philosophical and scientific arguments against an absolute or universally objective morality are overwhelming creates thus itself a serious problem in moral motivation. This is, in fact, the difficulty that makes the crisis of our time in a very special sense a value crisis. It should be clear, after the horrible experiences of the recent past, with perhaps still more and worse to come, that one cannot maintain a civilization worth maintaining when nothing is held to be right or wrong, or everything indifferently so. And it is only fair to say that this realization is one of the motives behind Dewey's demand for a scientific ethic. What he actually achieves, however, is something else again.

Denying that there are any ultimate, final standards to guide our particular moral judgments, Dewey asserts instead that each such judgment must be considered in terms of a concrete situation. (Concreteness, we know already, is one of the watchwords of the voluntaristic rebellion against reason!) Ends cannot be imposed *ab extra* but must arise out of the process of inquiry. (This, everybody knows, is "democracy" and also, alas, progressive education.) Every moral judgment is, according to Dewey, an assertion about what means are best used for a particular end, each end being, in turn, a means to another end, and so on, and so on. There are no final ends. One difficulty with this view is that which was pointed out bitterly by Randolph Bourne in his "Twilight of the Idols," namely, that, preoccupied as he is with means and anxious as he is to deny all final ends, Dewey failed to supply the generation of World War I that looked to him for guidance with a set of standards by which it could consistently behave. Bourne was right. And there are other difficulties as well. Let us grant that no value judgment should be judged without consideration of the particular situation in which it was made. Even so, what will be the criterion for deciding that one set of means is better than or morally preferable to another?

Dewey's answer, or one of his answers, is that every judgment of what is right or wrong is a plan of action in a concrete situation to be tested, like all such plans, by its consequences. If the consequences that result from the use of these means are satisfactory, then the moral hypothesis has been validated. We must know, then, when a consequence is satisfactory. According to Dewey, when it resolves the objective needs, interests, or conflicts of the situation itself. But what does it mean to resolve such things? Does it mean to maximize satisfactions? Or only those that are legitimate? Which and whose, among the several parties to a social issue, are legitimate? What, by the way, does it mean to maximize satisfaction? Anybody familiar with our tradition could easily multiply the questions. And he also knows that none of them has a scientific answer. What instrumentalism offers instead of an answer is merely a pseudoscientific, humanitarian-sounding verbiage. All that experiment and inquiry can tell us is what probably will be the effects of a certain course of action. A situation has no objective lacks or needs in itself but only in reference to the ends desired by men, and if men do not agree on their ends, no inquiry into means will ever settle the question.

The reason why Dewey so persistently overlooks this pat-ent truth is that he, like everybody else, does have a standard or a set of standards by which he judges which consumma-tion is preferable in any concrete situation. This standard, to be sure, is desperately vague, stated as it is in terms of adaptation, growth, and arrangements that favor adapta-tion and growth, with democracy as the political arrange-ment that best promotes all-around growth and change or, more grandiloquently, the capacity to "reconstruct" experi-ence. This is, in substance, a "democratic" version of the old romantic ideal of self-realization, as opposed to the Hebraic-Christian primacy of duty and self-sacrifice. While we need not argue here the respective merits of these ideals, we must ask how Dewey can believe that he has escaped what is for him the cardinal sin, the imposition of a fixed end on in-quiry. For it is apparently the quite definite and final end of his inquiry that anything prized as a result of reflection upon means and ends, causes and consequences, is good or morally desirable,[13] that all but spontaneous, unreflective choices are justified. To understand how Dewey can accept all this, one must understand his philosophy of reality.

Dewey set out to deny that there are any absolute, moral ends already given and to which we must conform. In order to do this, he denies that there is any hard fact, any uni-verse, moral or physical, given ready-made and to which we must also conform, though in a different sense of the word. Learning, according to him, is not a process of coming upon something already there; it is always interaction with the environment, and from this interaction what we come upon is made or emerges. Until these changes take place there is nothing to be known or learned. Likewise, the application of scientific method, as Dewey conceives it, always results in

[13] The reader will have noticed that I just played fast and loose with the ambiguity of "end." But so, characteristically, does Dewey.

some changes in the world. To know is to act; and all acting produces change. Changes brought about by experimenting with means to ends are, on this view, the essence of both scientific and moral action. And these changes also *are* the values. There are no others. Thus, just as truths are man-made, not in the trivial sense that when we alter something in the world a proposition which was once false is now true, but in the curious sense that we have made an event true by, in the ordinary usage, discovering that it is true, so values also are man-made, are products of the process of inquiry. Unitary, unbifurcated reality is, for Dewey, this ongoing sociobiological process. Out of it both fact and value, or what we ordinarily call so, emerge. Also, as long as inquiry proceeds scientifically, change in the right direction is guaranteed, for, by definition, values are the outcome of inquiry. By thus identifying value with whatever results from the scientific manipulation of society, Dewey convinces himself that his own values are not imposed, that they merely tell us, scientifically, all about the natural ways of value.

Perhaps all this will become a little clearer if we consider two historical parallels. The absolute idealists, it will be recalled, objectified values by identifying them with the succeeding phases in the undulatory unfolding of the Absolute, its final synthesis or realization being, accordingly, the highest value. The social Darwinists, on the other hand, projected the value into social evolution by optimistically conceiving of this process as a progress. Dewey cannot accept either of these rationalizations. He rejects absolute idealism because of the unempirical, transcendental character of its Absolute. Spencer's more naturalistic view is unacceptable because it discourages attempts to improve the human condition, by its notion that one cannot interfere with the social process. In other words, Dewey rejects these two process philosophies because of the inevitability of their processes, leaving no room for the "creative intelligence" of man. So he replaces Hegel's transcendental Absolute and the social Darwinists' self-propelling evolutionary development by the sociobiological process of inquiry. Since values emerge from this process, which is most efficiently carried out by the scientist, science can tell us not only what is the case but what ought to be the case. What this amounts to, if the democratic and scientific verbiage is shorn away, is this: the one true standard by which to judge ideals is that whatever comes later in time is better than what precedes it. So we are urged to believe that in a world sufficiently plastic the future cannot but be better than the past. All we need do to assure this is always to be doing something instead of passively contemplating and accepting a world already there. This activity itself is its own direction; novelty is improvement; new experience is growth; growth is its own justification.

The process of inquiry within the system is not only the creator and carrier of all values but it also affords the means for Dewey's other end, the resolution of all the traditional philosophical problems. The distinctions or dualisms between mind and body, reason and experience, appearance and reality, fact and value, and, most fundamentally, subject and object or knower and known, are the source of these problems. The way in which a philosopher analyzes these distinctions determines his metaphysical position. For Dewey, the problem is elementary. Not only are all such analyses a waste of time because they are of no practical import, but they are even intellectually unnecessary. The traditional dualisms are all denied by the simple expedient of viewing them as mere aspects or artifacts of the process of inquiry which will all disappear when, if that were not im-

possible, the process has run its course. All attempts to consider these aspects apart from their context in inquiry are
"viciously abstractive" or, in Dewey's most common term
of abuse, mere "formalism." This, of course, is in itself a
metaphysical position. Despite its naturalistic trappings, it
is in essence idealistic, for it denies any sheer given element
in experience, fact and value alike arising as inquiry creates
them from the "indeterminate situation."

When one thus penetrates to the metaphysical core of this
philosophy, it becomes difficult to understand how it could
be so influential. But it is a truism that when a philosophy
becomes popular only its more immediate implications are
seen and understood, while its logical structure and its metaphysics remain obscure. The instrumentalist insistence upon genetic explanation and social context, upon freedom of
inquiry and freedom to change, was all that was seen of this
philosophy. Up to a point, these principles had a most salu-
tary effect upon economics, law, education, and history, although, to be sure, Dewey was not alone responsible for the
"liberal" and "progressive" developments in these fields. Be
that as it may, institutional economics, the new history, and
the legal realism of Justice Holmes, all helped correct many
errors and abuses. But even these limited instrumentalisms
became self-defeating when faced with such problems as the
choice of moral standards by which the law is to be judged.
Or, in the case of institutional economics, if abstraction from
the total social context must not be made, it becomes virtually impossible to know anything at all about the economic
factors as such.

Literature, both critical and creative, also felt the impact of instrumentalism. Literary history was no longer to
concern itself with the artist and his work considered in
isolation but with the relationship of literature to its total

social and economic environment. Vernon Louis Parrington's work, with its social interpretation and evaluation of literature, is the finest flower of this movement. The radicals in literary criticism—Van Wyck Brooks, H. L. Mencken, Waldo Frank, Max Eastman, John Reed—wanted an empirical criticism which would bring literature closer to economic and social realities, make it directly relevant to social reform. Novelists like Upton Sinclair, Frank Norris, Theodore Dreiser, and James T. Farrell were themselves imbued with the belief that literature must have a direct social function, that, in particular, it is its duty to depict the evils and abuses of the social system, to dramatize the external conflicts between man and his social environment rather than the private and internal ones between man and man or man and himself. Again, the parallels with the Marxist theory of literature are as painful as they are obvious.

Most profound and lasting, perhaps, is Dewey's influence in the field of education. *Democracy and Education,* one of the many books he devoted to the subject, applied his philosophical views to this crucial area. Since it is "undemocratic" to impose anything from the outside and since personal growth is the only value, the child is not something to be educated or instructed. Rather, it is the job of the educator to ascertain the child's own interests and, having ascertained them, to supply the conditions for their satisfaction. Since learning always involves doing and doing always involves changing, education is to be the process of making over the child's environment for the satisfaction of its needs and desires. Since practical problems are the only real problems, the school must not be a place set aside for learning lessons but must duplicate the home and community life, teaching, to whatever extent it teaches any subject matter, what is useful there. Since democracy involves co-operation, all competitive activity, such as examinations, is to be discouraged. Thus society is, quite unrealistically, adjusted to the child. But, on the other hand, since social integration is the means to growth par excellence and since mind develops in the process of integration and adaptation, adjustment of the child to the society is the paramount concern of the teacher. The school, generally, should not isolate itself from the community; it must directly aid in the resolution of social conflict. What was perhaps originally primarily a protest against the rigid curricula of the past and an unreasonable emphasis on rote learning has since become a rationalization for teaching less and less.

And how confused all this is, into the bargain. On the one hand, the environment is held to be all-important in determining what a person is like; on the other, it is believed that the child has in himself, without external stimulation or direction, interests and purposes for whose satisfaction the various subjects are merely means. Education is to have relevance to later participation in the life of the society. Society, even the most democratic, is full of competitive struggles and tensions of one kind or another. Yet, in the instrumentalist school all is to be co-operative. One of the greatest human motives, to learning as to everything else, the desire to excel, is left completely unused. Is it, perhaps, that emphasis on the intellect is "aristocratic," that differences in sensibility and intellectual ability are "undemocratic"? For the classical conception of democracy as a bill of rights and as equality of opportunity is subtly reinterpreted into a drab egalitarianism. Combined with emphasis on doing, on the practical, on the satisfaction of needs, this suspicion of mind, this ill-concealed dislike of everything excellent has, as we all know to our sorrow, produced the most anti-intellectual system of education, whose main function is adjustment and, by some strange logic, the facilitation of social change. Since the difference between fact and value is blurred, the values which really inspire this educational system go unarticulated and unacknowledged. Not knowing where fact leaves off and where value begins—are they both not aspects and outgrowths of the process of inquiry?—the "Deweyan" educators in all honesty do not realize that, if they have it all their way, indoctrination toward mediocrity and conformity will soon have taken the place of education.

v—The Analytical Turn: *(1) Realism*

I mentioned before that various fields have shared in the thought pattern of Dewey's pragmatism. Legal theory, economics, history, psychology, literature, education, each and all had their respective revolts against what was variously called "formalism," "absolutism," "abstractionism," "natural law," "the past for the past's sake," "the genteel tradition," and so on. In each case, with minor variations, there is the same conviction that it is wrong, always and everywhere wrong, to treat any aspect of a culture in isolation from the total context. Also, men must not only, as passive beholders, plot the course of evolutionary change, they must actively help it along; truth, in economics, in law, in history, is a matter of social utility; ideas are valuable as weapons and as weapons only. All this is by now commonplace. For it is the essence of the American liberal tradition and it receives now daily its summing up,[14] nostalgically by the one side, mercilessly by the other. There is justice in either view. Yet, for better or for worse, what is thus blamed or praised

---

[14] See M. G. White, *Social Thought in America* (New York, Viking, 1949); Henry Steele Commager, *The American Mind* (New Haven, Yale Univ. Press, 1950); Daniel Aaron, *Men of Good Hope* (New York, Oxford, 1951); Trilling, *The Liberal Imagination.*

is the intellectual air we breathe—or it was. Why, for instance, this sudden rash of histories? A movement's history can be written only in perspective, when it has run its course, when it sinks into the past, not while it is still developing. In this Hegel was right. The owl of Minerva flies at dusk. And, indeed, the chroniclers of the liberal tradition write, or think they are writing, its obituary. Morton White, in his excellent book, writes of his protagonists as representing a generation that has passed. Henry Steele Commager, in his recent study of the American mind, notes, with obvious regret, that "co-operative instrumentalism" and the ideas associated with it have come to "seem outmoded and ineffectual." Lionel Trilling, the critic, speaks of the failure of the "liberal imagination." The wake continues and, I am sure, will continue for some time. In philosophy, too, mid-century America laments its lost innocence. But was it really so innocent? Let us see.

The gentlemen in mourning do not complain without cause. The names of Dewey, Holmes, Veblen, Robinson, Beard, and Parrington, do indeed no longer carry the emotional appeal they had. Their halos are tarnished. But they were liberalizing forces. Had they been the only such forces on the intellectual scene in the first half of the twentieth century, total pessimism would indeed be the order of the day. Fortunately, this is not so. Better than that, there were other forces, another movement. This movement may still succeed; it could conceivably achieve the ideals of the pragmatists where the pragmatists themselves failed. For this movement, these forces do not share the pragmatist's fatal weakness. In the person of William James, pragmatism represented in about equal proportions philosophy as analysis, as clarification of meaning and concern with fundamental questions about the nature of reality and philosophy as vision, as prophecy, as guide in life. As pragmatism developed into the instrumentalism of John Dewey, while the former did not entirely drop out, the latter, philosophy as a guide in life, became overwhelmingly predominant. More and more explicitly the aim of philosophy and the business of philosophers was held by the instrumentalists to be, as Marx said, not to *interpret* the world but to *change* it. The need for social reform seemed more and more urgent, the immediately practical more and more relevant, the theoretical correspondingly irrelevant and remote.

As the classical ideal of philosophy as contemplation fell into disrepute, as the sense of mission grew, instrumentalism and the liberal movements associated with it in the special fields became self-defeating. Everything was staked on a faith in progress made possible through the "creative intelligence" of man. Basing its social idealism on a wish and a hope rather than on a sober understanding of things as they are, pragmatism began to crumble as an active force as soon as its basic unanalyzed assumptions came into conflict with the new science of man. This science insists reason is not the master but rather the servant of the emotions. The events of the recent past devastatingly supply the evidence. And, faced with the bitter facts of the dark side of human nature, the liberal tradition began to totter in its utopian foundations. The pragmatist apostles of science and of what they took to be its method tried, and are still trying, to shut their eyes to the facts, scientific and otherwise. An ironic fate indeed for these innocent worshipers of science. In other camps, we see men retreating from social optimism into a despairing pessimism. From a humanistic religion based on devotion to man's needs here and now, many are turning for solace to medievalism or neo-orthodoxy. Art and literature witness the rising cult of irrationality. But these recent deserters from the liberal tradition are, for the most part, the young, the less firmly rooted, the inheritors rather than the formulators. The elder statesmen among the pragmatists and their followers now take, as I just hinted, what is in a sense an even more desperate stand. They refuse to acknowledge that anything has happened, that anything has changed. They stolidly reaffirmed and continue to reaffirm their fundamental convictions, bewailing the "failure of nerve" of the deserters from the liberal camp, reasserting their faith that men need only to use their intelligence freely for all to be well. But what avail such counsel when the very science one has been taught to revere teaches that men will not *be* rational, that, moreover, man and all his works are just an incident in the long biological chain of cause and effect? So, bitter and disillusioned, increasing numbers of our intellectuals turned and are turning their backs upon the false prophets of an impossible utopia. Liberalism—the empirical, pragmatic, forward-looking tradition—seemed and still seems to have reached a blind alley.

A famous nineteenth-century philosopher once remarked that "where all is rotten it is a man's work to cry stinking fish." Clearly, there is something rotten here. Nor is the stinking fish hard to find. Its "head," if it may be so called, is the assumption, unhappily shared by the now budding historians of our recent tradition, that the decline of the pragmatic, reformist, socially orientated movement betokens the demise, in America, of all thought that stands for the classical liberal ideal. This assumption, in turn, has complex origins. Partly, it stems from the mistake of taking the reformers at their own valuation as the only bearers of the liberal cultural tradition. Partly, and more fundamentally, this unfortunate assumption that liberalism as a political and human ideal can find no help from current philosophic and scientific thought arises from a failure to adequately analyze and understand the meaning and significance of the developments in the so-called "new science" and "new psychology." More than this, if the pragmatically orientated tradition had not itself failed to ask the necessary fundamental questions and to make the corresponding clarifications, it would not today be in its twilight hour, it would not have failed its adherents so abysmally when the need was greatest. Unfortunate as this is for them, it is fortunate, for the high social idealism they so sincerely espoused but so inadequately based, that they are not and never were alone on the intellectual scene. At about the same time as the instrumentalists in philosophy were winning wide support, both public and academic, for their program of single-minded devotion to the cause of social reconstruction, other philosophers were less sensationally but no less ardently going about their seemingly less urgent business. While philosophy as vision and guide to life continued in the public eye, philosophy as clarification and understanding proceeded, without messianic fervor, to be influential in many fields. Side by side with the instrumentalist, pragmatic tradition and frequently engaged in controversy with it was the group best known today as the analytical school. Though in the meantime influenced by British and Continental developments, this school, too, has roots in native soil.

The pragmatists, following James, had attacked the absolutistic aspect of objective idealism, at the same time preserving its subjectivist, voluntaristic features. The new realists[15] had no such romanticist scruples. They undermined idealism at its foundation. By refuting idealism—the view

[15] This movement reached its height in 1910 by the publication of the "Program and First Platform of Six Realists," signed by E. Holt and R. B. Perry of Harvard, W. T. Marvin and E. G. Spaulding of Princeton, and W. B. Pitkin and W. P. Montague of Columbia. Two years later a co-operative book, *The New Realism* (New York, Macmillan, 1912), was also published.

that the world is the creation of mind or action—the Absolute Mind is shown to be only an extension of the original absurdity to the infinite. Doctrinally, there was nothing new about the new realists. It was, just as its proponents insisted, a return to the natural or naïve realism of the man in the street to whom the world is as it appears to be, who believes that we perceive things as they really are. Such realism had been the official philosophy in our colleges for the first three-quarters of the nineteenth century. The older, so-called common-sense or Scottish realism, however, was religious in its motivation, holding that we could know spiritual and moral truths about the existence of God and the soul with the same direct apprehension we had of physical objects. For evidence, it appealed to established beliefs.

The new realists, though many were theists, were naturalistic in their analysis of man and his relation to the world. Following James, in one of his more naturalistic moments—for, in his concern for the freedom of the will, James tended to waver on the issue—they denied a spiritual soul, holding that consciousness as well as its objects were part of the natural processes. Ralph Barton Perry, of Harvard, was probably one of the most influential among the new realists. The basic fallacy in idealism, as he conceived it, was that it argued from the redundancy that anything known or thought is known or thought by somebody, to the significant and quite different proposition that nothing can exist independently of being thought, known, or perceived. But the new realists were all, each in his own way, concerned with this fundamental tenet that, contrary to idealism, knowledge as such makes no difference to the objects known, that the latter exist antecedently to being known just as common sense tells us they do. There was also a secondary reaction, as it were, against the bifurcation of nature we are already familiar with. Science seemed to deny reality to the secondary qualities, to the colors, tastes, odors, sounds, and textures of the world. This was intolerable. So the new realists, converting the idealist thesis, held that *all* the things of ordinary experience were non-mental, in the sense that they exist independently of any perceiver. But in order to hold this it was necessary to bridge the gap between the mind and the physical world, to show how those aspects of experience which were clearly related to the act of perception could also exist independently of it. In the light of the science of perception, this might seem an impossible task. But William James had suggested what seemed a way to do the impossible.

James's 1904 essay "Does Consciousness Exist?," which I have discussed before, marks the beginning of systematically developed realism in America, though realistic articles, including some by the many-faceted James himself, had appeared even earlier. James's one-stuff theory or neutral monism makes the content of consciousness, the mental element, identical with the physical object. Its being mental or experienced is simply one relation the object has to a percipient body. In another relation, the same object is physical. My typewriter as I see it and pound it is part of my consciousness and, in that relation, mental. At the same time it is also on the table and, in that relation, physical. The relation the typewriter has to me when I perceive it, like the one it has to the table, is an "external" one, that is, it remains what it is despite its relationships either to me or to the table; it would still be the same machine if related to another perceiver or another piece of furniture. This asserts at least what the idealists explicitly denied when they held that knowledge, being an "internal" relation, was constitutive of its objects. James's theory that consciousness is composed of the same elements as the rest of the world, only in different combinations or relations, permitted the realists to explain how the qualities are both out there and in the mind and how different people can observe the same object. This is very pat, for it seems perfectly commonsensical to say that we know the physical world as it really is by direct awareness, an immediate apprehension of the object. Unfortunately, it is too pat. A moment's thought reveals that common sense is fraught with perplexities. *With these perplexities all analytical philosophy begins.* For, consider: If I see objects directly as they really are, what about the stick that looks bent in water or the tracks that appear to converge? Note that we say the stick *looks* bent and the tracks *appear* to converge, not that it *is* bent or that they *do* converge. We know perfectly well that this is not the case. Then don't we see the object as it really is? If not, what is it that we see? Is there something that intervenes between our percept and the object? If so, what and where is it? Among other more recondite difficulties, the new realism was notoriously inadequate to account for the occurrence of error and illusion. Its merit was that it rediscovered, and thus recovered, the classical tradition of Western philosophy.

A new group was not slow to point out the errors of the new realists. Accepting the neorealistic insistence on the independence of knower and known, this group repudiated the doctrine of immediate or direct knowledge of physical objects. Instead, they held that our beliefs about physical things were mediated by inferences from immediately given mental states or ideas which "represent" the objects. Roy Wood Sellars, of Michigan, one of the most active members, in 1916 christened the doctrine of the group "critical realism,"[16] to distinguish it from the naïvetés of its predeces-

---

[16] The realist controversy was climaxed in 1920 by *Essays in Critical Realism* (London, Macmillan), a co-operative work by George Santayana, formerly at Harvard; C. A. Strong, formerly at Columbia; A. K. Rogers, formerly at Yale; A. O. Lovejoy, at Johns Hopkins; R. W. Sellars, at Michigan; J. B. Pratt, at Williams; and Durant Drake, at Vassar.

sors. This new view was much more in accord with the scientific theory of perception, which teaches us that the mental image is the result of an interaction between the physical object, light rays (in the case of a visual image), and the physiological, neurological optical structure of the perceiver. Hence, also, the possibility of error, for which, since it occurs, philosophers must be able to account. We might be having a hallucination when we believe that there are really pink elephants out there. In the inference from the mental state to an object, the critical realists placed the source of error. Critical realism, to be sure, has problems of its own. If only the idea or percept of the object is ever given, never the object itself, how do we know that the ideas correspond to the objects, or, more devastatingly, how do we know there *are* any objects? While the new realists were charged with being unable to account for error, they returned the compliment by asking how their opponents could account for knowledge. The controversy between the two forms of realism fattened the journals for the first quarter of the century, finally drifting into a peace without victory, each side concentrating on the problems posed by their respective positions regarding the relationship of the mind to the external world.

However, the realists' answers need not detain us. Their importance lies elsewhere. First, a series of very real intellectual if not very practical problems were rescued from the oblivion to which the pragmatists would have abandoned them as outmoded, artificial, and even politically suspect. By their concern for the fundamental issues, the realists happily prevented the liquidation of the philosophical enterprise. In this they also had to insist, and fortunately they did insist, on separating philosophy from its history. (Idealists, for reasons of their own, did not stress the distinction.) Philosophy, they held, must not confine itself to commentaries on the classics. If philosophy were but the history of philosophy, it would have no history. The idealistic belief that the history of philosophy as such throws more light on any problem than a new, direct, and independent analysis does is a superstition. Furthermore, under the influence of science in general and of new developments in logic and mathematics in particular, the realists adopted a philosophical method that time and later refinements have proven to be eminently fruitful. They issued a manifesto appealing to philosophers to slough off the anti-intellectual habit of appealing to feeling or a peculiar illumination that is presumably vouchsafed to philosophers alone. They prescribed, in particular, a scrupulous use of words as a basic canon of intellectual integrity; rhetorical flourishes must give way to the pursuit of exact meanings so that no doubt remains about what is being said. To sharpen the issues, to be explicit about agreement and disagreement, the prejudice against analysis shared by both the pragmatists and the more mystical visionaries of the Whole must be abandoned. We do *not* "murder to dissect." Wholes must be intellectually broken up into parts, not for dissection's sake, but in order to better understand the way in which the parts were indeed related to form a whole. Analysis, to be sure, is not an end in itself but an access to reality. A philosopher must not assume, without having previously convinced himself by analysis of the soundness of this assumption, that there is an all-sufficient, all-embracing principle, a single fundamental proposition that adequately explains or determines everything. It *might* be true that moral or spiritual principles dominate the world. It *might* as well be true that mind is causally inseparable from its social and biological contexts. But if a realist should come to hold either of these views, he will have arrived at it by reasoning that has high regard for logical form, whose meaning is manifest, whose evidence is clearly marshaled. More specifically, the realists advocated and defended at length, against their idealist and pragmatist detractors, the method of logical analysis, the use of semimathematical or logical techniques for intellectually breaking a whole into its component parts, as a sharper tool and, in fact, as the only tool available for the resolution of certain types of philosophical puzzlement. For the most part, it was a younger generation of philosophers who were to reap the fruits of this method during the last fifteen years or so. For it took some time to learn how and where to apply the tools and, it must be confessed, we still had something to learn from England and the Continent.

On any roll of the critical realists the name of Santayana inevitably appears. Yet he has insisted that his system is "no phase of any current movement,"[17] dissociating himself from his former colleagues as emphatically as he had many years earlier dissociated himself from all things American. In a sense, there is justice in his claim to uniqueness; in a sense, there is not. One need turn only a few pages of the lush, Pateresque prose of Santayana to understand why, as soon as he found it feasible in 1912, he shook the dust of Harvard and America forever from his heels. Here is definitely an exotic. Yet, a bare summary of the philosophical views imbedded in what is, for the modern taste, a rather too self-consciously literary prose does not reveal the heart of the strangeness. His basic philosophy or metaphysics is of the commonest—a rather uncompromising materialism.

The source of his charm for many is not just in the ca-

---

[17] *Scepticism and Animal Faith* (New York, Scribner, 1923), p. viii. This book, an introduction to the four-volume *Realms of Being*, is the best summary of Santayana's philosophy.

dences of his lines; Santayana does not share the lack of sensitivity, the hostility toward the imagination that mar and limit so many materialists and naturalists. On the contrary, he believes that the works of the imagination alone are good, all the rest "ashes in the mouth." In more than one way, Santayana is himself one of those "private gentlemen," he somewhere mentions, whom the clergy and the professors cannot deceive. He is, of course, responsible for the famous epithet, "the genteel tradition."[18] Like most of his historical expositions, the essay in which he introduced that phrase is an acutely insightful dissection of the psychological bases and cultural role of the philosophy of an era. Born in Spain of Spanish parents, reared, by fortuitous family circumstance, in Boston, he always remained the worldly-wise, disabused, and disenchanted Latin aristocrat. He is as impatient of Protestant moral preoccupation as he is of the egocentric romances of idealism and of American industrial society. All, all alike are futility; only the aesthetic awareness of the realm of essences makes life worth living.

Yet these essences do not exist; only matter exists. Essences are what is immediately given to spirit, yet spirit does not exist. It is but an efflorescence of material mind or psyche. As a consequence of the acts of material mind —sensing, thinking, remembering, imagining—the essences are intuited. Being the whatness or characters of things, they are ideas or universals. Intuition is the contemplation by spirit of these mental aspects of material impressions and sensations. Santayana is thus what is known as an "epiphenomenalist"; all the furniture of the mind is but the causally sterile emanation of matter. Since Santayana's matter is, in fact, the sphere of cause and effect, and since matter alone

18 "The Genteel Tradition in American Philosophy" in *Winds of Doctrine* (New York, Scribner, 1913).

exists, the essences cannot therefore exist. They are merely signs or symbols of existing substances or things. Even that they are this we must take on animal faith, as a belief to be justified only pragmatically. For there is a complete and un-bridgeable gap between essence and matter. Only essences are given in experience, though history, science, and psy-chology all rest on the assumption that there are things in-dependent of us. On this assumption Santayana, too, rests.

Since only essences are ever given, all systems are symbols, but scientific systems by an act of animal faith refer to outer fact, and only such reference is knowledge. All other sym-bolic systems, like poetry and religion, are mere intuition of essences, which is never knowledge. They are the myths man's fancy weaves among the essences, having no reference to the natural world of events. "Religions are the great fairy tales of the conscience." His sympathy toward religions is thus aesthetic, not moral. It is the drama they embody that appeals to him rather than their ethical imperatives. In this conception of the moral life, the "Life of Reason," the limi-tations of Santayana's sensibility reveal themselves. Like the ancient Greeks, he only asks how man shall live to be happy, recoiling from the Protestant's "agonized conscience." Yet he is not quite disenchanted enough. Or perhaps he is just dated. To pursue the Life of Reason, he thinks that we need only establish a harmony of the impulses; natural happiness is at hand if we but order the forces in human nature. The oppressive shape of duty, of obligation toward others, no-where casts its shadow over Santayana's realms of being. Not surprisingly, then, the ideal is neither the pursuit of knowl-edge nor goodness, but the aesthetic contemplation and ma-nipulation of evanescent essences, the Life of Spirit. For the world-weary grandee who "knows," this and only this is the good life.

vi—The Analytical Turn: *(2) The Last Fifteen Years*

An impressively written and impressively argued two-volume work that appeared in 1939 was received in many quarters with some astonishment. Brand Blanshard's *The Nature of Thought* was a detailed and up-to-date defense of absolute idealism. The appearance of this work, its form, and the startled response it evoked are all indicative of the present temper of American philosophy. The spirit of the Absolute is among us again, but as yet it is something of a sport in the English-speaking philosophical family of the day. Two things about Mr. Blanshard's work are above all characteristic of his time and place. The first is that although it is admittedly a restatement of nineteenth-century absolute idealism, nowhere is there any reference to Spirit, God, or the Absolute. The pervasive religious tone and slant of Royce's works is completely absent from Blanshard's. This is not an accident, nor does it imply anything about Blanshard's personal religious beliefs. I do not know anything about the latter, nor are they relevant for his philosophical position. Blanshard himself, quite obviously and very significantly, does not consider them thus relevant, while the nineteenth-century idealists most emphatically did. The second symptomatic characteristic of his defense of idealism is that Blanshard devotes specifically two full chapters and many more scattered pages to the discussion of views associated with the Cambridge school of analysis and the logical positivists. And although Blanshard's discussion is highly critical, his method nevertheless reflects the tremendous influence of analytical philosophy on the present generation of philosophers of whatever metaphysical stripe.

In 1903, G. E. Moore, at Cambridge University, published two very influential works. "Refutation of Idealism," a rather short paper, established realism in England. *Principia Ethica,* it is probably not too much to say, has influenced almost everything written on ethics since. In the same year, Bertrand Russell, also at Cambridge, published his *Principles of Mathematics,* which contained much of philosophical and logical interest and greatly influenced, among others, the American realists. In 1910, Whitehead and Russell published the first volume of *Principia Mathematica.* They thus established definitely the new discipline of so-called formal or symbolic logic which, having slowly developed since the middle of the nineteenth century, is a tremendous enrichment and extension of the classical logic of Aristotle, and more than that. In 1922, Ludwig Wittgenstein, a Viennese who had been a pupil of Russell, published his oracular *Tractatus Logico-Philosophicus,* enunciating some of the fundamental positivist views. A year later I. A. Richards's and C. K. Ogden's *The Meaning of Meaning* appeared, and in 1924, Richards published his *Principles of Literary Criticism.* These names and dates tell the story of an interaction between two philosophical movements, British and Continental, which has determined the complexion of a great deal of recent American philosophy. As the mention of Richards indicates, the same interaction has greatly influenced recent literary criticism in America. This conjunction seems less odd when it is pointed out that all these philosophers share the linguistic approach to the problems of philosophy.

American philosophy from Emerson to Royce and James drew upon European sources. The nature of the recent impact, however, is much more direct. For after the debacle of the thirties many European philosophers who survived it came either to England or to America. And many contemporary philosophers here, of all kinds, have been influenced by this dispersion. Our intellectual contact with England having always been close, young American philosophers went over in droves during the last quarter of a century to find out what was going on at Cambridge and, as the new movement spread, at Oxford as well. Or English philosophers were invited to America as visiting lecturers, and some stayed. The ground here had been prepared by the realists' revolt, and as this movement lost its vigor, the new developments and the new blood came to the fore, helping to maintain an intense philosophical interest.

The students of the most active realists in the first two decades had inherited a respect for method on the one hand and what seemed a philosophical blind alley on the other. Their elders had fought to a standstill the issues between the new realism and critical realism. If the debate were continued in the old terms, nothing new could be said. Men like C. I. Lewis, of Harvard, had taught the younger generation the new logic, but its usefulness for philosophy was only vaguely realized. The British and Continental developments provided a fresh approach to metaphysical problems and, at the same time, a field of application for that powerful tool, the new logic.

All analytical philosophers[19] have in common a stress upon the importance of linguistic analysis for the solution of philosophical problems. Philosophers from Plato on have been concerned with clarification of meaning; in this respect current analytical philosophy merely continues that aspect of the tradition. But what has so far been subsidiary, however important, now becomes central. Analyti-

---

[19] The number of philosophers in America who could be classified as analysts is so great that I have decided against listing any. Virtually every major college and university has its representation. A journal devoted exclusively to analytical philosophy, *Philosophical Studies,* is edited by Herbert Feigl and Wilfrid Sellars.

cal philosophers hold, by and large, that all philosophical problems arise from the fact that our ordinary language is ambiguous, containing within itself, collapsed as it were, level upon level of discourse. To be sure, ordinary language serves us well enough when we want to make just ordinary statements about the world, either commonsensically or as scientists. But as soon as we turn philosophical and begin to worry about such things as the difference between reality and appearance, the existence of other minds, the relation of a knower to what he knows, or the nature of truth, we shall be led into paradox unless we are careful to make distinctions that are buried in the grammar of everyday speech. This has an important consequence. The classical tradition, which includes the American realists, holds that philosophical disputes are over matters of fact, to be settled by appeal to fact. Analytical philosophers hold that the controversies between the various metaphysical positions, such as between idealism and realism, far from being about things or facts, arise from the inadequate analysis of words or language and are, in this sense, verbal. Philosophers who are worried, for instance, about the existence of other minds or of the external world have all the relevant information at hand: our everyday experience. What is needed is clarification, not new information. It does not follow, however, that philosophical problems or propositions are verbal in the sense of being trivial. For the underlying assumption, without which the concern with language would indeed philosophically be trivial, is that the structure and logic of our ordinary language is significant and not arbitrary. We use the language we do use because it fits, in some sense, the world in which we live. This view, common to all analytical philosophers who are not merely engaged in interesting linguistic parlor games, combines the ideas of G. E. Moore and Wittgenstein. G. E. Moore insists that, in order to be able to speak philosophically about reality, existence, or goodness, we must first understand, meticulously and accurately, what common sense means when it says that tigers exist, or that chairs are real, or that honesty is good. Wittgenstein's emphasis is on the thesis that language is a map of reality, that the structure of our language mirrors the structure of our world. Thus the study of the logical or grammatical features of our language can give us insight into those pervasive or categorial features that are the philosopher's concern. All this is not strange but is familiar even from literature. In his influential *Practical Criticism*, I. A. Richards addressed himself to the question of how it is that, despite the backwardness of psychology, we do manage to say some very subtle and recondite, yet true, things about our feelings. How is it that we know so much about ourselves that has not found its way into textbooks? The answer he found in language:

Put shortly, the answer seems to be that this knowledge is lying dormant in the dictionary. Language has become its repository, a record, a reflection, as it were, of human nature. . . . If we could read this reflection of our minds aright, we might learn nearly as much about ourselves as we shall ever wish to know. . . . We should certainly increase enormously our power of handling our knowledge. Many of the distinctions words convey have been arrived at and recorded by methods no single mind could apply, complex methods that are, as yet, not well understood.[20]

If language is the repository, the reflection of human nature, it is also much more. For the world consists of more than just human beings, and our language has had to deal with all the rest as well.

[20] London, 1929, pp. 218–19.

Although analysts frequently speak of grammatical clarification, the philosophical use of that term is much broader than is customary, covering subtle features of logical structure that ordinarily escape us. The philosophical significance of the new logic lies in its power to uncover just these subtle features. In ordinary grammar, for example, the two sentences "Hamlet is fictitious" and "Shakespeare is English" have the same form. If one uncritically accepts this common grammatical form, it is easy to get into a glorious philosophical tangle. Certain realists concluded that, just as there is (ignoring tense) a man Shakespeare who has the attribute of being English, there must also be somebody called Hamlet who has the attribute of being fictitious. Hence, Hamlet in some sense exists yet is fictitious. By using the new logic, Bertrand Russell was able to achieve grammatical analysis that eliminates this absurd conclusion, by showing that "fictitious" is grammatically but not logically a predicate or attribute. Similarly, by confusing the various logical functions of the verb "to be," the idealists were able to "prove" that whole and part are different yet the same, that subject and object are different yet identical, that, in fact plurality is illusory and everything is One. Again, linguistic clarification showed that one need not resign oneself to paradox.

The analysts' clarification of meaning should not be confused with anthropological and psychological linguistic studies. Analysts are not concerned with the historical origins and social functions of language but with its logical structure and the meaning of certain terms which the plain man does not use at all or not in a manner that leads to perplexity. Material object, reality, appearance, substance, knowledge, truth, meaning itself, are all terms which ordinarily do not puzzle us. The problems and paradoxes arise when we begin to reflect about these things, and one purpose of philosophical analysis is to remove the puzzlement. To ask about the nature of the real or of the good in a philosophical sense is not, according to the analysts, to ask for factual information but to ask for a clarification of language, for an analysis of the meaning of the terms. Once such an analysis has been provided, it becomes, of course, a matter of fact to determine what things are real and what things are good. Furthermore, if the structure of language reflects the structure of our world, then the kind of analysis of these terms which a philosopher gives determines the kind of philosophy or metaphysics he has. Whether or not a particular philosophical system or linguistic structure is adequate or a true and exhaustive map of reality can only be determined by each individual for himself in terms of his own experience. If, however, one believes that philosophy should offer a complete description of the fundamental features of *our* world, then an analysis which violates our experience, whether by denying the importance of the feelings or emotions, or by asserting that what we ordinarily consider real is really illusion, is either an inadequate map of our world, or false.

Fundamentally, the term "analytical" designates a technical approach to the problems of philosophy, a taking of them for their own sake, which may or may not involve the use of a special language. The use of logical tools is merely a refinement of the technique in the interests of precision both in statement and in solution. The problems are classical: the ultimate nature of knowledge and reality; how and what we do know; the meaning of truth, goodness, and beauty; the nature of justification in matters of morality, our ethical standards, as well as in matters of fact. The analytical philosophers have in common only an approach and a method. Their solutions may and do vary in all possible directions. This is sometimes obscured by the fact that one particular group of analytical philosophers has received a great deal of attention, not to say notoriety. I refer to the logical positivists.

Any living movement is difficult to characterize, but this is perhaps especially true of logical positivism, or logical empiricism to use the name some positivists prefer to distinguish their school from nineteenth-century Comtian positivism. Like pragmatism, positivism lives on more than one level. In the first place, there is a characteristic set of attitudes or *Weltanschauung*. Then, there is a specific group of doctrines which may be said to define a minimum positivistic position. After this, there is a penumbra of doctrines which are neither logical consequences of the minimum position nor are held by all who would call themselves positivists. However, if it is the better part of wisdom to bow to common usage, then possibly people who do not hold these associated doctrines of the first or last category should not call themselves, or be called, positivists. The positivistic temper of mind is in many ways similar to that of the instrumentalists or pragmatists: it is naturalistic, humanistic, scientific, and optimistic. This common temperament was one of the things that led, in the thirties, to a *rapprochement* between European positivists who came to this country and the Deweyan pragmatists. Another was that they both, though in different ways, "eliminated" traditional metaphysics. There are today still individuals who hold a mixture of positivist and pragmatist views, but in the main the differences between the two schools turned out to be sharper than that *mariage de convenance* could bear. For, the instrumentalist's geneticism, his intense hostility toward analysis and toward all formal or technical studies as well as his belief in the social engineering function of philosophy, are all, among other things, at variance with logical positivist conceptions.

Logical positivism, like the realist movements here and abroad, was a reaction *against* the prevailing absolute idealism of the second half of the nineteenth century. The early Continental positivists were also strongly opposed to the Kantian view that we could have knowledge about the world without experience. Positivism was a reaction *to* the new developments in physical science, mathematics, and logic, and many of the early positivists were trained as scientists and mathematicians rather than as philosophers. While the pragmatist and the late nineteenth-century attitude toward science generally tended toward a simple, whole-hearted acceptance of its findings, the positivists were concerned with a clarification and critique of the fundamental concepts and methods of science. As philosophers of science, in this technical sense, they have made many remarkable contributions to the understanding of the relativity theory, quantum mechanics, probability theory, geometry, the foundations of mathematics, and the nature of scientific explanation and method in general. Consonant with their interest in the foundations of science and in the integration of scientific knowledge, they have formed an Institute for the Unity of Science which publishes the *International Encyclopedia of Unified Science,* a two-volume series of twenty monographs on various aspects of science and scientific method.[21]

Possibly one of the most influential consequences of the positivistic interest in clarification of the fundamental concepts of science and mathematics was the development of the

21 Many technical papers by members of the group have appeared in *Philosophy of Science,* a journal founded in 1934 and now edited by C. W. Churchman in collaboration with Gustav Bergmann and Henry Margenau.

discipline known as "semiotics," or the theory of signs and languages. Interest in the analysis of meaning and of language is, of course, not exclusive with the logical positivists. The term semiotics, for the general theory of signs and the way in which they function, was taken over from John Locke by the American, C. S. Peirce, William James's friend, as far back as 1867. Said Peirce:

The woof and warp of all thought and all research is symbols, and the life of thought and science is the life inherent in symbols; so that it is wrong to say that a good language is *important* to good thought, merely; for it is the essence of it.[22]

But Peirce's work remained virtually unknown until the publication of his collected papers in the 1930's, and by that time the study of language had proceeded apace. Psychologists, anthropologists, and literary scholars had also shown a new interest in language. But, in recent times, it has been men associated with the positivistic movement who have done the most systematic work on a science of semiotics.

Charles W. Morris, an American associated with pragmatism, contributed to the *International Encyclopedia* the widely read *Foundations of the Theory of Signs,* an exposition in clear, relatively popular terms of developments in semiotics up to that time. Morris distinguishes among three "dimensions" of semiosis: syntax, semantics, and pragmatics. Syntax deals with the relations of linguistic expressions to each other; semantics, with the relation between the symbol and its referent; and pragmatics, with those between a language and its users. A work of literature may, for example, be studied in any or all of these three ways. Concern with what is called the "internal consistency of a poem" would involve a mixture of syntactical and semantic consid-

[22] *Collected Papers, op. cit.,* Vol. II, Par. 220.

erations, the relations of the expressions to each other and to what they speak about. Analysis of the multiple meanings, connotations, implications of a term in context would also involve these two dimensions of language. Studies of the effect of the poem on readers or its relation to the author belong to psychological pragmatics. This shows also that the three dimensions are not independent of each other. Pragmatics presupposes syntax and semantics; semantics presupposes syntax.

There are, I think, three doctrines that may, with some historical justice, be said to form the minimal positivist position, though whether a philosopher holding only these doctrines in common with other positivists should be called by that name is, as I indicated before, a verbal issue. These basic doctrines are: (1) All of our knowledge about the world stems from experience. Hence, since experience is always fallible, factual knowledge is never certain. The only certain truths we know are those of logic and mathematics, which are true by virtue of their meaning alone and, in this sense, not factual. (2) We have no knowledge of real connections between different things, different characters, or different facts. This was Hume's basic point. (3) The traditional philosophical problems arise from verbal confusions and disappear, therefore, in a properly clarified language. These problems are, therefore, "pseudo problems," that is, while they appeared to deal with questions of fact, they were really only questions about language. This is the essence of the positivists' famous "elimination" of metaphysics, which they share with other analytical philosophers. However, certain extensions of this doctrine commit them to more than many other analytical philosophers are ready to accept.

Like all analytical philosophers and like the pragmatists

before them, the positivists attempted to establish a "criterion of meaning," a rule for deciding under what conditions a statement is meaningful. Stated broadly, the positivistic "verifiability theory of meaning" holds that a statement is meaningful when we know what we would observe if it were true and, also, what observations would falsify what it asserts. This is essentially Peirce's pragmatic principle, which we discussed before. (The positivists, however, do not, as did James and later pragmatists, identify truth with verification. Theirs is strictly a verification theory of *meaning*.) Under this criterion, many of the assertions of traditional metaphysics become "meaningless." "Nothingness penetrates the universe; pure being and pure nothing are therefore the same"; "the world of experience is unreal"; "the Absolute enters into, but is itself incapable of, evolution and progress"—these are some of the illustrations the positivists like to quote. For none of these assertions is there, as they stand at least, any possible observational test by which to decide whether they are true or false. Since statements of this kind do turn up again and again in much of traditional metaphysics, particularly of the idealistic variety, "metaphysics" unfortunately became a pejorative term with the positivists. Strictly, however, the rejection applies only to a special way of talking about the most fundamental, and that is the metaphysical, issues. There has never been any controversy among empiricist philosophers about the need to limit discourse to what could be tested by experience. To accept this principle one need not be a logical positivist. However, later on the criterion was changed so that an entirely different class of propositions allegedly also became meaningless.

The positivists, unlike the analysts who derive from G. E. Moore and, in many respects, from Wittgenstein, were primarily concerned with science. It was in the light of this preoccupation that Rudolf Carnap propounded his doctrine of physicalism, according to which all statements, including those of psychology, are meaningful only if expressed in the language of physics. This makes all statements about mental events, like love, hate, fear, moral experience, memories, thoughts, acts of belief and imagination, meaningless if they are taken literally. To become meaningful, these statements and the concepts that occur in them must first be construed behavioristically. Behaviorism, the doctrine that all mental concepts can be defined in terms of observable behavior, makes good science; but it is questionable philosophy. Common sense knows that to say a man is in love is to say not only that he behaves or would behave under certain conditions in a certain way but also that he has a specific feeling or state of mind, which only he can observe. If, then, philosophy is to be a *complete* and undistorted description of the fundamental features of our experience and our world, then it must start from what is directly given in experience instead of merely reconstructing it behavioristically from what we know less directly. And what is so directly given to us are our mental states, whether these are our perceptions of the external world, our emotions, or acts of our minds. The positivists' preoccupation with science and physical objects leads thus to a narrow, quasi-materialistic conception of empirical fact. Here again we find that same suspicion of mind that we have traced since James. And, using metaphysics not in the pejorative sense but simply in the classical sense of one's view of the nature of reality, this is itself a metaphysical position. But this is not to say that if meaning is defined in terms of immediate experience, what William James called knowledge-of-acquaintance, a complete rather than an impoverished description of the world along positivistic lines could not be given. In this respect, the work of Gustav Bergmann is, perhaps, the most significant development within positivism during the last decade. On science, including the science of psychology, Bergmann takes a strictly positivistic position; but in the theory of knowledge he rejects all scientism and attempts to do justice to the subjective elements of experience, including the ethical and the Self. The more orthodox positivists think, therefore, that Bergmann is a metaphysician; he considers himself, probably rightly, a positivist in the tradition of Wittgenstein.

The belief of many positivists that a complete description of the world can be given in terms of physical objects alone is, in many subtle ways, related to attitudes that are then ascribed to all positivists and which arouse much hostility, as I see it, not without reason. For such a doctrine and such attitudes leave the world desolate of mind. But there is another thesis often associated with logical positivism which achieved even greater notoriety and aroused even stronger resistance. This is the emotive theory of value.

All empiricists, positivistic or not, make a distinction between judgments of fact and judgments of value, between what is and what ought to be. And all empiricists, positivistic or not, are relativists with regard to value. That is, they hold that there is no one absolute standard that holds for all people at all times and in all places, independently of human needs and desires. To say that much, however, is not to have analyzed correctly our ethical and aesthetic judgments, which are as much a part of our experience as is whatever we perceive of the external world. The question what exactly it is that we mean when we say of an act that it is good or of a poem that it is beautiful thus remains open. A well-known positivistic analysis was presented by Richards and Ogden in their *The Meaning of Meaning;* by Richards in other works; by the Englishman, A. J. Ayer, in his very widely read *Language, Truth and Logic;* and in a somewhat modified form by the American, Charles Stevenson, in his influential *Ethics and Language* (1944). I mentioned above that G. E. Moore's *Principia Ethica* had its influence on virtually everything written on value theory since 1903. He also coined a powerful slogan when he first spoke of the naturalistic fallacy. Moore, who is not a positivist, showed that any attempt to define the ethical concept "good" in terms of a non-ethical concept, either "natural," like pleasure, self-realization, or some later stage in the evolutionary process, or "metaphysical," like supersensible reality, was doomed to failure. Any definition of "good" in non-ethical terms, natural or metaphysical, he therefore dubbed an instance of the "naturalistic fallacy."[23] Although his formulation of the fallacy has been subject to criticism, Moore adduced several arguments for his view that good is good and not another thing—arguments so impressive that for one generation, at least, no one, except the pragmatists, attempted to define the meaning of "good." Most positivists tried to define it *away.*

To achieve this feat, both Richards and Ayer used a rather specious distinction between the cognitive and the emotive functions of language. Language, it was said, serves a cognitive function when it conveys factual information, as in "our team won"; or it serves an emotive function when it expresses feelings, as in "hurrah!" A subjectivist ethical theory construes moral judgments as judgments about personal likes or dislikes. This turns ethics into a branch of psychology, for such judgments are obviously statements of psychological fact and may, behavioristically or otherwise,

23 See W. Sellars and J. Hospers, *Readings in Ethical Theory* (New York, Appleton-Century-Crofts, 1952), pp. 63–92.

be tested for truth or falsity. However, Moore had convinced everyone that such definitions do not do justice to that meaning of good, which cannot be identified with anything else. What, then, was the positivists' solution? Their physicalistic theory of meaning did not permit them to agree with Moore that there was such a unique quality of goodness. For such statements are not publicly verifiable, there being notorious disagreement in ethical (and aesthetic) judgments. The way the positivists chose to avoid the "naturalistic fallacy" as well as the acceptance of facts which are for them unverifiable was to deny that value judgments assert anything at all. According to the emotive theory, value terms are unanalyzable or indefinable, but this is not because they refer to some unique kind of entity, either in experience or in the external world or in both, but because they refer to nothing. They are semantically meaningless pseudo concepts, and the sentences in which they appear are pseudo statements, linguistic forms neither true nor false, merely expressions of emotion or expletives, like a cry of pain or joy.

Charles L. Stevenson, in his book, develops a theory which is a mixture of the subjectivist and expletive theories. To account for the motivational role of value judgments, he analyzes them into two components, one factual, one emotive. Thus the assertion "X is good" is translated into "I approve of this; do so as well." The imperative component points up the fact that ethical discourse is used in order to induce persons to change their value judgments. This disposition to induce changes in the hearer's behavior or attitudes is, according to Stevenson, the emotive meaning of the ethical judgment. Since direct commands are generally resented, the use of moral concepts, Stevenson maintains, is a subtle way of achieving the same effect. In 1926, I. A. Richards, writing in the same tradition, asserted that poetry consists of pseudo statements, expressions which were neither true nor false but which were justified by their effects upon our feelings and attitudes. To be neither believed nor disbelieved, they are instruments useful for ordering our attitudes to one another and to the world. Thus, on the emotivist theory, ethics, aesthetics, and poetry do not conflict with science, which is made up of publicly verifiable assertions, because they do not make any assertions at all.

The emotivist theory of value is a good escape hatch for a philosophy that holds that only statements about physical objects are meaningful. Yet it was probably more than a logical compulsion that led to this doctrine. Temperamentally, positivism like pragmatism belongs to the eighteenth century and shares that period's unbounded faith in man's rationality. Pragmatism, caught up in the evolutionist-idealistic trend of the nineteenth century, developed a metaphysics which ensures that values will emerge from the creative process. Positivism, growing out of mathematics and physics rather than biology, is too analytical in method and essentially too realistic in its theory of knowledge to share any such pseudo-Darwinian process-progress illusions. Much closer to the Enlightenment in its spirit, it reverts to the error of underestimating the moral and aesthetic aspects of man's experience. Thus, it does not realize that its account of these in terms of emotions, though genetically true enough, is intellectually inadequate and, therefore, culturally dangerous. For the distinction between the cognitive and the emotive is invariably made to the detriment of the latter. Values are "merely" expressions of emotion. This tendency to depreciate the irrational elements in man, joined to the belief that science can solve all our problems, has led many positivists to the facile faith that science can change human nature, to the shallow optimism that if we only change a few social and economic relations, everything will be well. Aside from its theoretical shortcomings, the doctrine that values are simply or merely expressions of emotions does not adequately reflect the importance they have in life.

Philosophically speaking, the distinction between the cognitive and the non-cognitive is systematically proleptic. James had already pointed out that on the level of direct experience, the starting point of all modern philosophy, this distinction does not exist. The sorting out, as it were, comes later. What is subjective and what is objective is not necessarily correlative with what is experienced or felt as being within and without. Nor, having determined what is subjective, or dependent upon us for its existence, have we thereby read it out of reality. So long as there are men with minds, love and hate, fear and conscience, and ideals and values will continue to be part of the total reality. Richards somewhere speaks of the "projectile" adjectives, like "gorgeous," "ugly," "beautiful," "pleasant," "good," terms that in some of their uses reflect a projection of feeling into external reality. Exactly. But *that* they are projected is not directly experienced. For this reason we may respond as strongly to these feelings as to those which further experience or intellectual analysis of our experience tells us are not "projected" but are of something independently "out there." It is not necessary to be false to the texture of our experience in order to deny absolute standards.

vii—Recent Philosophy and Literary Criticism

Literary criticism has shared the vicissitudes of philosophy in America. Both reacted against the genteel tradition. In each case the reaction itself took varying forms. In neither case can it be denied that the older tradition has continued here and there to perpetuate itself and occasionally even to show signs of vigor. In philosophy, idealism has risen again in the East and may stretch out even unto the prairies. The neo-orthodoxy of Reinhold Niebuhr and Paul Tillich and the interest in the Danish theologian-philosopher Kierkegaard have breathed new life into speculation, so that, while it is unlikely that the naturalistic trend will be reversed, it may on occasion meet with reverses. In literature, philological scholarship continues; sociological criticism in the manner of Parrington has still its devoted adherents. Doubtless all this is just as it should be. Yet, in both literature and philosophy a primary cleavage between two predominant tendencies may be discerned. In philosophy, those who believe that the perennial questions of philosophy are of value for their own sake are opposed by those who press for greater attention to urgent social issues. In literature, there are the literary historians and the "new" formal or analytical critics.[24] Analytical philosophers and the analytical critics have more in common than a name. As may be gathered from the role I. A. Richards has played in both movements, a direct connection between them, both historically and as to content, exists.

Richards, who was at Cambridge when Moore and Wittgenstein were there, visited frequently in the United States and is now at Harvard; he is generally considered the major contemporary influence on analytical criticism, his *Practical Criticism* of 1929 the major document. In this work, Richards insists that training is needed to read a poem; that poetry is a matter of communicated meanings, as open to analysis as is any other aspect of experience and communica-

---

[24] See William Van O'Connor, *An Age of Criticism* (Chicago, Regnery, 1952).

tion. To show all this, he uses in the most intensive manner the linguistic or semantic methods of analysis he himself had sketched earlier in *The Meaning of Meaning* (1923) and in *Principles of Literary Criticism* (1924). Richards and his student at Cambridge, William Empson, have influenced such eminent American critics as Ransom, Tate, Brooks, Warren, and Blackmur. Opposing the view that poetry, to be appreciated, requires only the proper spirit not intellectual effort, these critics all insist that to be appreciated poetry must first be understood; and that the key to its understanding is what the French call *explication des textes*. Analytical criticism as a return to the text is a triple protest —against impressionistic criticism, against the treatment of literature as a social and psychological document without proper attention to its intrinsic value, and against undue preoccupation with historical and philological scholarship.

The older tradition seeks to understand the poem or the novel by placing it in the context from which it arose. For this group, the political and religious attitudes, the mores, the economic conditions, the friends and lovers are indispensable for an understanding of the artist and his work. For the analytical critics, the relevant context is in, say, the poem. Their emphasis is on *what* is being communicated and the *technique by which* it is being communicated. The gloss, the close analysis of the text, are the tools. Meticulous attention is given to the poet's choice of words, to the order in which he places them, and to an interpretation of his imagery, often involving many refinements of verbal analysis. Analytical philosophers and critics both insist upon the importance of technique and upon the intrinsic value of their own fields. Social engineering and the history of philosophy as such are not philosophy, just as biographical studies and history of literature are not criticism. Analytical philosophers and analytical critics in many respects share the same method. A critic's analysis of the seven types of ambiguity and a philosopher's analysis of the seven meanings of the word "is" are very much the same sort of things; or, at least, more so than the surface chatter about the opposition between some catch-all positivism and poetry would let one suspect.

Yet, while adopting and refining Richards's method, many American critics have been highly critical of his theories on the nature of poetry, which were associated with his brand of positivism. The emotivist theory, since abandoned by Richards himself, particularly offended and was assailed by John Crowe Ransom and Allen Tate, among others.[25] This emotivist or pseudo-statement theory was thought to be patently unable to explain how an expression without content, asserting nothing, could determine attitudes or arouse emotions. If nothing is asserted, then there is nothing to be responded to. Ransom and Tate quite properly point out that there can be no emotion until an object has furnished the occasion for one, and that the effect of a poem depends, in this sense, upon its meaning. Besides, "emotive meaning" is a misleading name for the attitudes of approval or disapproval evoked by meaningful expressions. As in idiomatic speech, it is factitious to isolate one aspect of the cluster of meanings a term bears as *the* meaning. "Bureaucrat," "public servant," and "government official," if I may resort to a textbook chestnut, have an overlapping core of meaning, but their total meanings are different and not the same. These differences make the term pejorative, honorific, or neutral in effect and intent. But they do this not by them-

25 John Crowe Ransom, *The New Criticism* (Norfolk, Conn., New Directions, 1941); Allen Tate, *On the Limits of Poetry* (New York, Swallow Press, 1948).

selves but rather, in each case, in combination with the common core.

Nor did the proponents of the pseudo-statement theory pay enough attention to the grammar of poetry and all its differences from the grammar of either science or everyday speech. The devices of metaphor, trope, simile, figure of speech, and all the others must not, as we commonly say, be interpreted literally. And if no expansion of the metaphor, no paraphrase, is ever adequate, this merely goes to show that the linguistic conventions of poetry are not the same as those of ordinary speech. Words do not have meaning in isolation but only in context. Change the grammar, and the meaning changes. The unique grammar of poetry permits it to communicate several layers of meaning simultaneously, while ordinary language is too highly standardized for that. Probably this ambiguity is one major source of the aesthetic effect of poetry. The subtle structure of poetic language must, therefore, be understood. To promote such understanding is precisely the job of the critic. The later Richards recognizes and insists upon this. Hence, the great concern of the analytical critics with linguistic studies.

In an age of science, poetry, and not poetry alone, is on the defensive. The deprecatory phrase "mere emotion" has made the critics become concerned with the status of poetry as knowledge. Justifiably affronted by the philosophically spurious exploitation of the distinction between the emotive and the cognitive functions of language as it refers to the external world, they have at times been driven to claim a gratuitously mystical-sounding higher form of knowledge for poetry. If they mean what this seems to mean, they argue against their own argument that poetry is accessible to intellectual explanation. Scientist and poet alike speak of the world of experience. Velocity is no less and no more a part of my world than is greenness or love. In this sense there is no difference in their "ontological status." Yet, when Ransom says[26] that poetry has a unique "ontological" status, he means, as I understand him, that its subject matter, ultimately different from that of empirical science, is the "world's body," the full concrete richness and depth of the directly given, including the response of the beholder to what he so intently beholds. But a broader conception of empirical fact, suggested earlier, suffices to rescue the inner landscape from meaninglessness. There is no need to appeal to anything else that is, in some spurious sense, higher or, in principle, different. In the interests of finding laws, the scientist restricts himself to one class of perceptions, those which, because of these laws, we take to refer to something independent of us. The poet, primarily interested in what reverberates in the mind, does not so restrict himself. That is all. Once the insight is grasped that on the level of the directly apprehended the distinction between the cognitive and the non-cognitive does not exist,[27] the whole controversy about whether poetry is or is not knowledge loses its bite. By heightening *our* awareness of what is directly given to *him,* the poet both articulates and forms our moral and aesthetic perceptions so that we too may directly experience what would otherwise not be thus given to us. The pressure upon man of external reality and of scientific knowledge, the relationship between things-as-they-are and the world of the mind, is a recurring preoccupation of all art. This is the sense in which I understand Richards's oft-quoted statement that "poetry is the completest mode of utterance." An adequate theory of literary criticism, then, would seem to need

---

[26] Ransom, *op. cit.*, chap. 4. Also Austin Warren and René Wellek, *Theory of Literature* (New York, Harcourt, 1949).

[27] See above, p. 87.

not only the tools of linguistic analysis for understanding the text but also a grasp of the philosophical clarifications that can be attained through another study of language.

There has always been a division between philosophy as a guide to life or, as the pragmatists put it, instrumental to action, and philosophy as metaphysics, the search for answers to fundamental theoretical questions. More often than not the same men, as diverse as Plato and James, have engaged in both endeavors. Only in recent ideology-ridden times has the theoretical, contemplative temper been forced on the defensive. Just as there have been those who looked upon literature as nothing but the purveyor of morality or an instrument of social action, so, too, philosophy has been called to the barricades, as it were. Just as there is a feeling on the part of many literary historians that the analytical critics have carried the business of understanding literature a little too far, have become overly subtle, logic-chopping, and neglectful of the larger function of literature, so, too, philosophers have been accused of giving stones when men look to them for bread. In our time men value not ideas but ideologies, are anxious to hear not what there is but what they should do. So they overlook, in their haste, what the one can legitimately teach us about the other, namely, that there are some things men must decide for themselves. Apparently, this is a hard moral lesson to learn; yet it informs and pervades the human predicament. So it is surely not irrelevant as a guide to life. Among other things, it places responsibility squarely where it belongs. It is not from mere caprice that philosophers concern themselves with the meaning of "good" and with the nature of justification in moral and factual realms. Understanding the nature and limitations of knowledge may seem remote from the urgent social needs, yet it may make all the difference in the world between tolerance and fanaticism, between the timeserving of well-adjusted automatons and the fortitude and sensibility of those who have an inner source.

However, after all is said and done about the social functions of either literature or philosophy, and these are, of course, not inconsiderable, there remains the hard fact that both philosophy and literature are valuable in their own right, important and to be taken seriously for their own sake. To take literature seriously means to make an attempt to understand it, even at the price of arduous intellectual analysis. The perennial problems of philosophy have always required hard thinking as well as technical skill. To take philosophy seriously is to recognize these problems as important in their own right and, therefore, to recognize those special skills as worth acquiring. It is an encouraging sign that, despite all detractors, not a few American philosophers have continued and extended the tradition of taking philosophy seriously.

THE JOURNALIST AS LITERARY MAN

JAMES GRAY

THE writing habits of the journalist may be presumed to be partially unlike those of the professional man of letters. It is quite possible, of course, that the journalist sitting down to write a book will be influenced by what he knows or assumes to be the traditions of literary writing. He may allow himself more subtlcties of expression and strive for more universal truths than he would under the pressure or needs of his newspaper or magazine assignments. He may even think slyly or longingly about the possibility that his book will be selected by posterity as representative of its time and as containing truths cherished by all generations. On the other hand, the trained journalist necessarily brings to the writing of a book certain habits of mind and writing, certain feelings about the meaning of the term "objectivity," and certain devices for holding a reader's attention and for convincing him. If it may be assumed that he modifies his habits in undertaking to write a book, it may also be assumed that his own practices as a professional journalist have modified the literary forms—biography, autobiography, history, or criticism—in which he has written.

If his profession has influenced the way or the manner in which the journalist has employed traditional forms, it has also influenced his subject matter, what he chooses to write about. His chief subject, stated in the broadest way, is America: its past, as that helps us to understand present-day America; its foreign relations, as they help us to understand what we as Americans are and where we seem to be heading.

Americans in general were by no means sure, in the year 1900, that they knew even what they were. The idea of the youth of the nation was at once as fascinating and as inhibiting as youth always is to its giddy, easily embarrassed possessor. The idea of America's crudity had been insisted upon by European critics. The idea of its cultural dependence had been admitted by many of its own intellectual leaders. But in the midst of all this negativism of outlook there was a persistent impulse on the part of native observers to say something positive about the American way of life, not necessarily to glorify it, not necessarily to expose its frailties, not to accept commitment to a consistent program of analysis, but simply to assemble data about its enormous diversity.

This impulse was not self-conscious. To say that the theme taken up by a large bloc of writers was the rediscovery of America would be to suggest that a writers' congress had been assembled, that an official philosophy had been adopted, and that assignments had been made to individual researchers in many fields. Something no less absurd was actually to take place in the 1930's when the depression had made writing men conscious of the fact that they possessed the weapons of propaganda. But, at the turn of the century, what animated a significant group of American writers was the spontaneous impulse to record something of what they knew about their country.

These men, literary journalists most of them, did not have the techniques of the poet, the novelist, the dramatist, or the philosopher at their disposal. They depended upon wit, shrewdness of observation, interest in incident, and aptitude for perceiving patterns to make their great composite autobiography of America lively and revealing. Occasionally their group expanded to include, momentarily, a scholar on leave from the classroom or a creative artist taking holiday from his chief preoccupations. But, in general, the collaborators in this great enterprise were men and women who lived by writing for newspapers and magazines.

No one driving force animated the minds of all these writers. Many interests prompted their enterprises. They stirred the melting pot to see what had risen to the surface after a half century of migration. The muckrakers explored the neglected areas of husbandry of human resources and the hidden areas of the activity of exploiters of material resources. The debunkers undertook to deflate the superheroes. The ironists inspected the idiocies of the Jazz Age, while the angry prophets warned of serious threats to the solidity of American society. To tidy up after the collapse of the "American dream," during the depression enterprising workers of many kinds arrived with the equipment of the social sciences at their disposal. Two world wars provided opportunity for many writers to testify, each in his own way, that America, having achieved unity within multiplicity in its own government, must be the leader of the effort to achieve a broader unity within multiplicity on a global scale.

Throughout these fifty years, journalists have become more and more conscious of the desire to describe America, to define the variations of its character, to give to its humor, its customs, and its social graces their many local habitations and all of their American names. Into the broad current of American writing there poured studies of towns, cities, states, regions; of men, communities, special groups; of cults, movements, large-scale conflicts; of songs, legends, patterns of thought.

This obsession with the theme of "who we are" is almost the only thing that the literary journalists have had in common. They have written in frenzies of reproach and in almost equally aggressive frenzies of tenderness. They have written in ribald ridicule of patriots and with solicitous concern for the reputations of patriots. The tone of their work has sometimes alarmed conservatives, sometimes outraged radicals.

The big composite autobiography of America has examined democracy's bad moments without adequately accounting for them. It has made candid and sometimes exhibitionistic displays of flaws and foibles, seeming, with narcissistic fervor, to cherish and to caress its own weakness. Sometimes it has played the role of flagellant, whipping its own back in public. But the total effect of this account of trials and triumphs has been to call up an image of hearty confidence not unmixed with sentimental self-satisfaction, yet deeply imbued with the spirit of critical self-appraisal.

ii

First to offer testimony to the values of American life as they might be discovered in the course of the day's work were the foreign born. Their consciousness of problems of adjustment made them allies of reformers and, at the same time, prophets of optimism. Jacob Riis invited attention to both the positive and the negative aspects of his adopted culture in *The Making of an American* (1901), showing with naïve but agreeable cheerfulness how a man may escape from poverty, hunger, and the blows of policemen to become the friend of Theodore Roosevelt. The artless revelation of a generous nature was enriched by the further revelation that in Jacob Riis generosity had translated its impulse into action by helping to clean up slums and to alleviate sufferings from social inequality. Mary Antin's *The Promised Land* (1912) had the importance, claimed by its author, of being an utterance by one for many. The record of a Jew's escape, first, from the intolerable humiliations of life in pre-revolution Russia and, second, from the passive miseries of a Boston slum was marred by the homely heroics of an intensely self-conscious style; it was illuminated by the author's pure joy in acquiring the right of self-direction in a free society.

The idealism of foreign-born Riis, which did not permit him to forget the degradation of New York's mean streets, invaded the minds of native sons no less disturbingly. In the pages of McClure's crusading magazine and later in books, the muckrakers worked with cheerful defiance to earn as word of endorsement the epithet that had been flung at them derisively. In his *The Shame of the Cities* (1904), Lincoln Steffens carried into many communities the news of how sluggish voters had allowed cynical politicians to steal their birthright of freedom and to make a ribald farce of civic administration. The candor of Steffens's subtle intelligence made him the most brilliant of the muckrakers and at the same time the most unstable and least representative. His admirer, Oswald Garrison Villard, once described his writing style as "whimsical . . . elusive, fanciful and scoffing." Steffens's *Autobiography* (1931) and his *The Letters of Lincoln Steffens* (1938) reveal all the flashing facets of a temperament that Villard called "contradictory and paradoxical."

Much more typical were two other muckrakers, Ida Tarbell and Ray Stannard Baker. Miss Tarbell exposed the manipulations of monopoly so effectively in *The History of the Standard Oil Company* (1904) that John D. Rockefeller could speak of her only, with tight-lipped retributive scorn, as "that misguided woman." But she was always a sober patriot, who in her *The Life of Abraham Lincoln* (1900) had tidied up some of the legend-littered corners of her subject's early life. She found no contradictory irony in her celebration of *The Life of Elbert H. Gary; The Story of Steel* (1925), and when she came to write her autobiography in 1939 she called it, with grandmotherly serenity, *All in the Day's Work*. Just as idealism had conquered indifference in her bustling, housewifely attention to American problems, so faith had conquered doubt.

Ray Stannard Baker, who in *Following the Color Line* (1908) had been an eloquent and uncompromising opponent of racial inequality, became quite properly the analyst and appraiser of a progressive spirit in *Woodrow Wilson: Life and Letters* (1927-39). But what identified him as a remarkable product of American democracy was the fact that when he split his personality it was not into two roughedged neurotic halves but into two individualities, both neatly whole. As David Grayson, Baker wrote a long series of celebrations of the graces of American life, from a Tom Sawyer boyhood in Wisconsin on through the years. The first of these, published in 1907, bore the characteristic title *Adventures in Contentment*. Characteristic also of the ambivalence of the American writer toward the scene of his exertions is the work of Mary Heaton Vorse, whose autobiography *A Footnote to Folly* (1935) shows that despite biting criticisms made in the heat of conflict over labor problems, she never lost a feeling of sympathy for American society.

For a decade before the turn of the century the studio in which America sat for its portrait seemed to be the city room of the Chicago newspaper. At various moments in that period Eugene Field, George Ade, and Finley Peter Dunne wrote for the *Daily News*, the *Record*, the *Post*, and the *Journal*. The liveliness of their testimony to the diversity and, what seemed to them, the delectable absurdity of American life attracted large audiences and many imitators. Long after the "Chicago school" had been disbanded, its influence persisted, and interest in the satiric possibilities of the American scene may be dated from its activities.

It has been Eugene Field's curious fate to be remembered as a writer of the lachrymose light verse which was least characteristic of all the exercises to which his complex temperament prompted him. His newspaper column "Sharps and Flats" ridiculed Chicago mercilessly for the rawness of its commercial culture. He was a critic of insight and wit with many a memorable *mot* to his credit. (He once wrote of a performance of *Hamlet* that "Mr. ———— played the King as though someone else had just played the ace.") A lover of literature, Field was also the practical joke personified, and he once turned his genius for grotesquerie against himself by sketching his head, as "the Chicago Dante," wearing, by way of wreath, a ring of sausages. In him the frontier trail and the highroad of world culture met, and his facile improvisations had the significance of capturing something essential about the zigzag course of Midwestern writing as it made its way toward maturity.

George Ade suggested a very different aspect of the variability of American society. His *Fables in Slang,* published first as newspaper features and later in book form, were concerned with the eternal meeting of boy and girl, but their tone chastely eluded sophistication. The crucial problem was ever that of how money might be found to further the charm of boy meeting girl. But even as it was expressed in the language of overstatement, to which earlier American humorists gave so lavishly of their gifts, the love-making remained ingenuous. Shrewdness of observation was George Ade's asset. The kernel of truth was small, but it had a savory taste, at once tart and pleasant.

Finley Peter Dunne was the Chicago writer of most permanent value. Quite by accident he came upon a formula that served him well. What he wished to show was that Chicago, though it might be as raw as Field insisted and as parochial as George Ade suggested, nonetheless had a window open wide on the world. In the course of his daily newspaper work, Dunne created the character Mr. Dooley, who transformed saloon into salon for the discussion of international politics. Mr. Dooley spoke with a thick Irish brogue, for the imperfections of which his creator slyly accounted by saying that he wanted his mouthpiece to sound like an immigrant who had been seven or eight years in America and whose lingual innocence had been blurred, if not blemished, by Chicago. But what mattered, and what made Dunne a journalistic prophet ahead of his time, was the fact that, borrowing the immunity of the clown, he took highly effective shots at all the follies, grossnesses, and evils of world society. Among his subjects were the Dreyfus case, the reactionary decisions of the American Supreme Court, the grim tragicomedy of the Boer War, and the saber rattling of the German emperor. A man of subtle cultivation, with a passion for perfection in the use of words which matched that of Flaubert, Dunne managed to lend his gifts of grace to the utterances of an illiterate immigrant. He produced in *Mr. Dooley in Peace and War* (1898) and *Observations by Mr. Dooley* (1902) minor works of genius which, as one of his discerning critics pointed out, offer "a peep into the universal mind." The isolationists and America-Firsters of a later period would have had a serenely contemptuous enemy in Dunne. Though the successful calamity of being made comfortably rich by misguided benefactors finally robbed him of his impulse to write, he continued well into the century to influence America toward the acceptance of her proper place in world affairs.

Newspaper-trained writers explored the many aspects of the American scene far beyond the limits of Chicago. Often they produced works that were called novels because a slender thread of narrative held their anecdotes and observations together; but the true interest of these studies was simply that they offered glimpses of other Americas. Retiring from the service of Pulitzer to work at his own interpretations of American life, Irving Bacheller achieved venerability through longevity after being widely known by an American public for forty years. In *Eben Holden* (1900) and *Keeping Up with Lizzie* (1911), and also in his personal story *From Stores of Memory* (1938), he blended his mild-as-milk concoctions of nature lore, folk philosophy, and Yankee wit.

Edgar Watson Howe (Ed Howe to a wide audience) sent

out of Atchison, Kansas, the curious news of an America for which the ambivalence of a naturally critical intelligence expressed a crotchety distaste and a no less crotchety love. In *The Story of a Country Town* (1883), Howe had dramatized, with the greatest bitterness of spirit, the mean parochial temper and the devious malice of a society that suffered from a restricted outlook on the human problem. Then, with no apparent awareness of embracing inconsistency, he devoted the rest of his life (between unsuccessful bouts with fiction) to celebrating in the pages of his paper, the *Daily Globe,* the stern righteousness of commercial success. To work twelve hours a day, preoccupied with the immediate task in the day of small things, and to make this attention to duty pay—this was his religion. His command of a large following may be attributed to the fact that he contained within himself both the idealism and the willfulness of the American dream. His *Ventures in Common Sense* (1919) attempted to reconcile the opposites represented by the spirit of "getting along" and the impulse of social service. His book served to call attention to the strength and the weakness of the American dream at just the moment when its philosophy was beginning to be challenged by skeptical observers like Sinclair Lewis.

iii

The self-consciousness with which America had now begun to explore its past, present, and future was quickened by the whimsical influence of H. L. Mencken and George Jean Nathan as coeditors of *The Smart Set.* This magazine, established in 1890 to be quite literally the clearinghouse for gossip of the fashionable world, gradually had been transformed into a shelter on American soil for figures of

the great world of letters. Under the brief editorship of
Willard Huntington Wright, later to be the S. S. Van Dine
who blended aesthetics and murder so successfully in a long
series of mystery novels, *The Smart Set* introduced D'An-
nunzio, James Joyce, and D. H. Lawrence to the American audience. Mencken and Nathan, finding a place well
prepared for men who were informed about international
letters and who had strong preferences for originality and
boldness in the interpretation of the human condition, took
possession in 1914.

One of their chief contributions was to reclaim from neglect such American figures as Walt Whitman; another, was
to open their pages to new talent that showed signs of being
able to survive in the arena of letters.

Their exertions in search of novelty immediately attracted an attentive audience. This was in part because they lost
no time in launching a surprise attack on American values.
Each of the editors of *The Smart Set* had his own way of
making war on American complacency, but these ways were
equally destructive. The magazine became the forum of a
long debate of which the cheerful opponents never tired.
Was America, as Nathan insisted, a hopelessly dull place
which a transplanted *boulevardier* could endure only for
brief periods between flights to the refreshing fountains of
European culture? Or was it, as Mencken said each month,
an endlessly diverting five-ring circus in which creatures of
inexhaustible vitality and willingness, but with no skills of
any kind, persistently displayed their delightful ineptitude?
This gigantic burlesque of civilization bored Nathan and
sent Mencken into paroxysms of ribald laughter. American
patriots, overhearing at third or fourth hand the news of
these heresies, responded with exactly the outraged indignation that the Nathan-Mencken strategy was designed to in-

spire. By baiting the "booboisie" with a kind of schoolboy audacity, Mencken whipped American sensibilities. Each month, in a section of the magazine called "Americana," he gathered together all the evidences he could find of his country's fatuous, juvenile, insipid, and unimaginative self-love.

Inevitably, the irreverent and the high-spirited crowded about this leader, each eager to have a critical fling at native morals and mores. Biographers and analysts of the American scene were delighted with an opportunity to speak truth and to shame all the deluding devils of hypocrisy. Mists of adoration had hung too long about sacred heads and, at Mencken's prompting, brisk writers set out to dispel them.

So the debunking school came into existence. Mencken offered a kind of official endorsement by accepting the verb "to debunk" as a valuable contribution to the American language. He attributed its coinage to W. E. Woodward. But it is indicative of the true temper of the American experiment in self-appraisal that Woodward lived to repudiate the idea that he had led a stampede of idol-smashing. One of his novels *Bunk* (1923) had as its central figure a professional debunker, but he himself, Woodward insisted, never had been one. His book *Meet General Grant* (1928), often cited as the archetype of the debunking biography, was not intended by its author to be deflationary. In his candid, downright way Woodward sought only the truth, and he discovered in General Grant more of strength than of weakness. The portrait was affectionate, discerning, and, even in its determination to make full acknowledgment of flaws, tolerant. Indeed, it was a portrait very similar in essence to the composite portrait of American society that writers of the moment were putting together—rugged and resourceful despite the appalling threats to wholesomeness and inner security made by corrupting self-doubt.

Rupert Hughes, whose brief career as a journalist had deflected him from an early preoccupation with history into an orgy of improvisation as an author of trivial novels and a creator of pallid motion pictures, returned to research in 1926 with the first volume of his big study of George Washington. He, too, was called a debunker because, unlike earlier biographers, he did not have his subject live and move in the odor of sanctity. But his thoroughly conscientious and fully documented biography is still a valuable contribution to the shelf of journalistic exercises. Writers who entered the debunking school seemed very soon to graduate from it into serious efforts at appraisal; a few, of course, relegated themselves to a kind of debunking kindergarten where they amused themselves harmlessly and inconspicuously with feeble gestures of destruction.

The year before America entered World War I, it became evident that writers felt a disturbing obligation to restate the values of democracy. The question: What is an American? lay so close to the top of the native mind that the octogenarian Charles W. Eliot plucked it out to use as the title for an essay printed as the Introduction to Albert Bushnell Hart's *American Patriots and Statesmen*. It was in 1916 also that Mark Twain's *The Mysterious Stranger* was put into print at last and was discovered by one of his critics, George Soule, to be "straight from the soul of America," an interpretation of "the simplicity, the humanitarian aspirations, the reverence for the humble, the impatience of formalism, hard-headed distrust of authority, the resolute sensitiveness" that characterized Mark Twain's own temper and the temper of America. As though he wished his last will and testament to contain a repudiation of the false values of the American dream, Mark Twain had set down the admonition to youth: "Dream other dreams and better."

But these dreams were still to come. In 1916, "Americanism" had become a kind of state religion. The war in Europe, of which America hoped to have no part, had prompted certain writers to glorify the parochial ideal. In *American Patriots and Statesmen*, Hart praised the jingoes of native history with so unapologetic an air of rectitude that one of his critics accused him of identifying patriotism with the determination "to defy world foreign policy." Theodore Roosevelt, out of office but never willing to be pushed far from the center of the stage, published *Fear God and Take Your Own Part* in which he enunciated "the true principles of Americanism," finding these to be chiefly strenuousness and self-absorption.

Happily, these excesses of worthy sentiment were offset by more sober and discerning comments on what the duties, the opportunities, and the dangers of the democratic way of life might be considered to be. The posthumous publication in 1916 of the *Autobiography* of Charles Francis Adams revealed, with a racy candor that was new to the discussion of public affairs, how official Washington after the Civil War had vibrated, with characteristic American extravagance, between optimism and despair, while a puritan thinker looked on with a mixture of civilized amusement and blank misgiving. Albert Beveridge published, in that same year, the first two volumes of his *The Life of John Marshall,* which even in its uncompleted state established its author as the possessor of an ideal instrument for the measurement of values.

The impulse to put glimpses of the American scene clearly before citizens who had humbly supposed that landscapes, too, were something that occurred in Europe began to engage the attention of superior journalists in 1916. John Burroughs, the bulk of whose work had been done in another period, in *Under the Apple Tree* observed the patterns of nature and their corresponding patterns of ideas. His literary descendant and biographer, Dallas Lore Sharp, in books like *The Hills of Hingham,* undertook to encompass the infinite in terms of the immediate, small gratifications of American life. William Dean Howells, whose work as a novelist identifies him with the previous century, remembered his journalistic beginnings in his autobiography *Years of My Youth,* an expansion of the story told in *A Boy's Town.* A nearer approximation of the technique of rediscovery which became enormously popular in the 1930's was Theodore Dreiser's and Franklin Booth's *Hoosier Holiday.* Dreiser, turned journalist once more, still brought, as he had done in his prolix novels, the cataloguer's eye and the social worker's imagination to the task of describing a pilgrimage to the Indiana of his unhappy boyhood. With the artist-companion who illustrated the book, he theorized all the way about the plight of man caught between the pressures of indifferent nature and indifferent society. In this, as in his other work, Dreiser's earnestness begins by being exhausting and ends, paradoxically, by being both impressive and moving, so inescapably is his capacity for pity communicated to the reader.

Before World War I had written "finis" to America's analysis of itself as a kind of cultural suburb of Europe, representatives of the genteel tradition brought the art of urbanity to a fine, if not luxuriant, flowering on our soil. Samuel McChord Crothers, who seemed to be a Lamb lost out of his time and place, lent the faith of a liberal Unitarian mind and the grace of a gentle wit to volumes of essays called *Humanly Speaking* (1912) and, perhaps with unconscious self-criticism, *The Pleasures of an Absentee*

Landlord (1916). Agnes Repplier kept the informal essay alive almost without aid far into the 1930's as she wrote pungently about cats, tea, and Catholic heroes and heroines. In *Counter-Currents* (1916), the quarrel of her aristocratic spirit with what she took to be the disheveled manners and even more untidy ethics of modern society, took on a querulous tone. But her intent was to give witty reproof to shabbiness, and she was able always to demonstrate her exquisite right to do so. A writing brother of Agnes Repplier was Charles Macomb Flandrau, who produced few books, with long intervals of silence between efforts. His consideration of the tremendous trifles of human existence in *Harvard Episodes* (1897), *Viva Mexico!* (1908), and *Loquacities* (1931) made him, as Franklin P. Adams once observed, an "underwriter" of distinction. Flandrau, though he was the complete cosmopolitan, seemed less detached from his own country than did Crothers, for it was to the vagary of the American temperament that his urbane wit forever returned. Despite his acceptance of the genteel tradition and his long residence in England, Logan Pearsall Smith retained something of American audacity in his minuscule essays *Trivia* (1902) and *More Trivia* (1921). Smith reduced commentaries on certain kinds of delicate moral crises to sophisticated parables of some one hundred words each. His autobiography *Unforgotten Years* (1938) offered further notes to the story of the expatriate's pilgrimage begun by Henry James.

America's self-awareness may be said to have risen to the conscious level first in the minds of men who had been working long as novelists with the materials of the immediate environment. Hamlin Garland from the year of his birth in a log cabin on the Wisconsin prairie had identified himself with the Middle West. Its scenes were the scenes of his

stories of pioneer privation, hardihood, and homely hero-
ism. A liberal in the terms of his time, he had written with
uncompromising candor about every aspect of the effort
to create a way of life in a harsh, though often rewarding,
world. Then, in 1915, having renounced the hope of making Chicago the artistic center of America, even with the
help of Henry B. Fuller, Lorado Taft, Harriet Monroe, and
William Vaughan Moody, he moved to New York and began a new career. The journalistic studies in autobiography
were the result. From the vantage point of his success in the
new project, the world of Garland's youth looked less wintry
and formidable. *A Son of the Middle Border* (1917) and *A
Daughter of the Middle Border* (1921) presented the village, its people and its affairs, in the mellow afterglow of
opportunity seized, and of courage exercised, triumphantly.
Garland exercised the pioneer's skill in improvising a new
technique for handling new materials. He had anticipated
the regionalists who were to borrow heavily from him a few
decades later. His two important interpretations of American life were among the few vivid works of a period comparatively barren of such interests.

Though one or two novelists, Willa Cather and Edith
Wharton among them, were doing some of their most important work in this period, the great company of the past
was beginning to fall away. The uncertainty of the moment
that followed America's entry into World War I did not
immediately encourage the development of new writers. An
end had come, in 1918, to one phase of American literary
history.

The Education of Henry Adams, previously printed in a
private edition of only one hundred copies, was given to
the general public for the first time in 1918. Adams's sense

of failure as a product of the great tradition of education, his complete inability to make his peace with a commerical society that had taken the dynamo as its god, probably corresponded very little with the sense of dissatisfaction that stirred in the minds of most of his readers. His rejection was too exquisitely complete to be matched by many Americans, whose chief asset is their adaptability. Yet the civilized grace with which Adams suggested that the time had come to re-examine all the elements that go into the training for maturity spoke to a sizeable company of readers, giving them a not unpleasant sense of being heretics by proxy. All over America, in colleges, in studios, in every place of meeting for men and women who were not completely infatuated with American opportunity, *The Education of Henry Adams* was discussed with the spontaneous enthusiasm of people who wished to "dream other dreams and better." As though to emphasize Adams's thesis, Van Wyck Brooks, in *Letters and Leadership*, set before Americans the challenge: "We wish to play our part in the higher life of the world but we are incapable of doing so because we have no organized higher life of our own."

Appropriately enough, the year in which Adams's and Brooks's books were published proved to be a peculiarly barren one for American non-fiction. The political observers were at work trying to help America digest the experience of the war—the ubiquitous Theodore Roosevelt in *The Great Adventure; Present-Day Studies in American Nationalism,* Elihu Root in *The United States and the War,* Mark Sullivan in his study of sea power *Wake Up America.* But for a general interpretation of values, the reader had to be content with novelist Meredith Nicholson's engaging but vague *The Valley of Democracy,* which suggested that the French settlement of the Mississippi Valley had established principles of co-operative effort which that region must for-ever hold sacred.

The lag between the shock of recognition that a new phase of American life had begun and the effort to give expression to that awareness was, after all, comparatively short. The year 1920 was marked by the emergence of certain writers who brilliantly illuminated a variety of American themes. Though the year 1920 is remembered chiefly for *Main Street* and *This Side of Paradise,* it saw many other significant appeals for public attention. Sherwood Anderson and Willa Cather were enlightening their audiences with *Poor White* and *Youth and the Bright Medusa.* T. S. Eliot and Carl Sandburg, who had been offering their very different invitations throughout the teens of the century to any who wanted a new view of poetry, began now, by the very persistence of their efforts, to claim consideration as creative artists. It was a good moment for the American writer because there had come together a reasonably large company of men and women who wanted to hear what he had to say and granted him the full right to speak his mind as he chose. Theodore Dreiser, for example, in *Hey Rub-a-Dub-Dub,* allowed the lowering clouds of his pessimistic philosophy and of his threatening rhetoric to brood over America and to conclude that it was highly neurotic. It was a moment when everyone was trying to write the same study of a nation's adolescence and, though there were as many prescriptions as there were journalist-diagnosticians, still, the cause of self-understanding was served.

The serious journalist settled down in 1920 to the task of acting as amanuensis to a newer America, helping to get its story down on paper in all the wide and wild diversity of its interests. The last of the disciples of the American dream of getting-along had his word. In *The Americanization of*

Edward Bok a magazine editor reduced the success story to absurdity as, with the greatest gravity and in the third person, he rehearsed his effort to set up a capacious shrine to utter banality. William Du Bois, the most highly disciplined and skillful of all America's Negro writers, spoke in *Darkwater* with the bitter-brilliant clarity of his outraged idealism for the rights of men and women whom democracy had timorously and cynically rejected. Upton Sinclair, remembering his youth as muckraker, clamorously, and often upon too little evidence, challenged the ethics of editors in *The Brass Check* (1919). George Creel anticipated America's broadening awareness of its role in global affairs in his study of Woodrow Wilson called *The War, the World and Wilson*. Champ Clark, who had once hoped to edge Wilson out of his hope of reaching the White House, offered in *My Quarter Century of American Politics* a new model for the recounting of a serious career as public servant.

Clarence Day, who was presently to emerge as the ironic yet tender interpreter of a way of life that could have developed only in America, made his literary debut in 1920. *This Simian World*, the most fastidiously brutal of satires, suggests ruefully that a less apelike creature than man might have made a better job of creating a livable life on our globe. More soberly, Katharine Fullerton Gerould in *Modes and Morals* found Americans lacking in reticence and decorum.

John Lomax, one of the first students of our regional cultures, began collecting *Songs of the Cattle Trail and Cow Camp* with a proper awareness of their value as part of the native heritage. Constance Lindsay Skinner, later to give design to an important project in regional study, anticipated the spirit of this adventure by contributing to the Yale University Press series, *The Chronicles of America*, her fine studies *Adventurers of Oregon* and *Pioneers of the Old Southwest*.

All these books—critical or uncritical, characterized by extravagant hope or by brooding doubt—shared the purpose of putting clearly before a people who had become curious about themselves the themes and scenes of their native life.

During the 1920's these interests continued to engage the attention of serious writers who addressed themselves to the popular audience. The very embodiment of this impulse was James Truslow Adams, who gave his talents to the task of making a complete re-examination of the puritan way of life. Splitting the difference between exhaustive scholarship and readable drama, he produced a trilogy on the early days of the American experiment—*The Founding of New England* (1921), *Revolutionary New England, 1691–1776* (1923), and *New England in the Republic, 1776–1850* (1926) —studies which did much to clarify traditions that had tended to drift off into the realm of myth. With a tireless and indeflectible sense of direction, exploring the major intelligences of early American history in an effort to uncover the roots of belief, Adams selected and edited *Hamiltonian Principles* (1928) and *Jeffersonian Principles* (1928) and wrote *The Adams Family* (1930). The last of these books was no labor of filial devotion, for the author himself was not of this branch of the Adams clan. Other large works, *The Epic of America* (1931) and *The March of Democracy* (1932–33), extended Adams's contribution as a celebrant of the virtues of industry and the sacredness of common-sense conservatism.

The compulsion to get American stories told prompted a group of writers, who found that they could not record quite everything in the form of fiction, to resort to public confession. Theodore Dreiser, Sherwood Anderson, and Ludwig Lewisohn, who shared an acute distaste for the cramping limitations of our business civilization, produced autobiographies that were designed to shock the bourgeois citizen out of his complacency. The American way of life, these former journalists said, in effect, was by no means as tidy as its official spokesmen pretended. Dreiser's *A Book About Myself* (1922) and *The Color of a Great City* (1923) suggested that the average man was able to take little satisfaction from the stereotyped pattern of the American dream. Anderson's rejection of part of American life was balanced by the highhearted acceptance of affirmative values; his *A Story Teller's Story* (1924) contained the author's own brand of idealism as an implacable enemy of spurious ethics and second-rate hopes. Lewisohn's criticism of American culture in *Upstream* (1922) was too heavily freighted with personal complaints against the academic world to be acceptable as an impartial discussion.

Biographers were preoccupied with American figures. William Allen White, long since established as the sage of the *Emporia* (Kansas) *Gazette,* wrote one year about *Woodrow Wilson, The Man, His Times and His Task* (1924) and the next, about *Calvin Coolidge* (1925). The flexibility and indulgence that made White so variable an endorser seemed in the end, to the writer himself, like the babbling testimony of softness. But at the moment, his universal benignity toward anything that could be represented as ideal brought him a large audience. White's popularity had the good effect at least of concentrating attention on the problems of democratic government.

Claude Bowers, a good man to have about when tasks of a high order in journalism or diplomacy were being assigned, produced an able study of Jefferson and Hamilton in 1925. Allan Nevins, while he was still a practicing newspaper man writing editorials for the New York *World,* published his thorough and judicious review of the career of *Frémont, the West's Greatest Adventurer* (1928), later revised and enlarged (1939) as *Frémont, Pathmarker of the West*.

Most conspicuous among the journalistic popularizers of themes from American history was Carl Sandburg, who published in 1926 the first two volumes of his monumental study of Lincoln. *Abraham Lincoln; The Prairie Years* won the respect of historians for the thoroughness of its research and the sanity of its judgments; the work won the affection of the casual reader for the charm of its anecdotal treatment and the creative sympathy which brought Lincoln to life.

The themes of American life were not exhausted by these interests. In 1924, Gilbert Seldes subjected *The Seven Lively Arts* to serious study, offering the first suggestion made by a responsible critic that America's contribution to creative expression on the screen and the radio must be examined as an influence that showed every sign of being both permanent and pervasive.

American economic practices did not, of course, go unchallenged. Taking up the arguments against the divine working of the laissez-faire system that Thorstein Veblen had put vigorously before American readers, Stuart Chase began his career, in 1925, as a popularizer of technological principles with his book *The Tragedy of Waste*.

The desire to rediscover every aspect of the undisciplined urgency that surged through American life took writers up many bypaths. James Stevens began to explore and exploit native folklore in his stories of *Paul Bunyan* (1925). Walter Campbell (Stanley Vestal) took up the story of his native West. The former Rhodes scholar found no themes so rewarding as those stored away in the balladry of the Southwest region and in the personal histories of its conspicuous figures. Campbell enriched the autobiography of America with many sound, authoritative, factual accounts like that contained in his *Kit Carson* (1928). Lyle Saxon mixed courtliness with impudence to achieve a new kind of literary grace when, in 1927, he became a kind of official chronicler of the South in his *Father Mississippi* and, a year later, in *Fabulous New Orleans*.

In 1923, Mark Sullivan, who worked at journalism throughout his active life, began a bold project which was to put a clear and detailed picture of American civilization before students of the immediate moment. The six volumes of *Our Times* discussed every aspect of life in the first quarter of the century, from politics to taste in women's dress. This formula for preserving the pleasures, pastimes, and pressures of a period became steadily less sprightly, but the final result is of value to social historians. *Our Times* caught in its very style the temper of the times; it was brisk, expansive, optimistic, critical, and uninhibitedly opinionated.

Another typical product was *The Great American Band Wagon* (1928), the work of Charles Merz, later to be editor of the *New York Times*. Searching, ironic, yet essentially affectionate in his appraisal of American values, Merz suggested that the American band wagon, for all its jolly blatancy, was not a bad vantage point from which to view the world.

Events of the 1920's brought an end to some of the treasured myths of which the success story was the buoyant but thoroughly boring product. Only a few writers had anticipated the crisis with which the era was to end. They trooped through the year of the fall of Wall Street still bursting with *élan*. Indeed, the literary season of 1929 was a lively one. James Truslow Adams celebrated the virtues of *Our Busi-*

ness Civilization. That strenuous journalist Herbert As-
bury, who had spent the decade looking for American saints
and sinners of whose activities he could make mildly audacious sport, got around finally to writing a life of Carry
Nation, who crusaded violently for righteousness as though
she had mistaken herself for the embodiment of the church
militant. Claude Bowers discussed, more in sorrow than in
anger, the mistakes of the post-Civil War period in *The
Tragic Era; The Revolution after Lincoln.* Marquis James
emerged as a skillful and conscientious journalist-historian
with *The Raven: A Biography of Sam Houston.* Dreiser
paid doleful tribute to *My City.* Ludwig Lewisohn continued to make his elegantly phrased complaints in *Mid-
Channel.* George Seldes accused Americans of allowing their
right to freedom of expression to be stolen from them; his
book was called, with characteristic irony and belligerence,
You Can't Print That! His milder brother Gilbert pursued
his task of hollowing out a niche for American art with a
study called *The Movies and the Talkies.* Walter Francis
White reminded us sternly that we hadn't even begun to
cope with the problem of racial cruelty; *Rope & Faggot; A
Biography of Judge Lynch,* despite its inflaming title, had
the virtue of offering a sober, relentless indictment of bigotry. Maurice Hindus anticipated the preoccupation of the
next decade with problems of foreign relations; *Humanity
Uprooted,* a study of the Russian experiments in collective
farming, helped to persuade America to look beyond its own
borders in an effort to foresee the problems of the future.

Most striking of all the publications of that significant
year was Waldo Frank's *The Re-Discovery of America.* Here
was the familiar theme again, but it was presented this time
in a different manner. The workaday journalists had looked
at America with shrewd, appraising eyes; the tone of their

comments, though often critical and ironic, was essentially downright and direct. Frank brought to his discussion the tone of the prophet; the exalted lyricism that had run through all his books was particularly conspicuous here. The "aesthetic vision of life" on which Frank prided himself added an almost tremulous quality to his appeal for a finer effort toward the realization of essential American ideals, those of the spirit.

iv

The decade of the 1930's began, inevitably, in a mood of questioning. What had happened in Wall Street, followed by the reverberations across the continent, launched a period which the journalists helped to make intensely sociological in its preoccupations. The old certitudes had proved to be dusty, indeed, and doubt was everywhere. Some of the more volatile creative artists seemed to surrender their intelligences hysterically to the influence of propagandists for other ways of life. The type of novel and play that came to be known as "proletarian" urged the necessity of making a complete job of rejection and of inaugurating a new start. The serious journalists felt no such impulse. They continued to examine values under new and more powerful searchlights of criticism, but they felt no inclination to throw out a system along with its outmoded practices. Typical of the temper of the 1930's was Walter Millis's *The Martial Spirit; A Study of Our War with Spain* (1931). The book's candid protest against forces that had sent the United States headlong into the adventure of the Spanish-American War persuaded some critics that the author himself was a jingo isolationist, and Millis was long in living down this undeserved reputation.

The most completely native products of the sociological decade were books like Mary Roberts Rinehart's autobiography, Frederick Lewis Allen's backward glance at the 1920's, and Constance Rourke's study of American humor. Mrs. Rinehart's *My Story* (1931), much finer in quality than any of her popular novels, offered a candid account of a life that was sustained by a genius of competence. The author's progress toward success in her profession (or professions), in her marriage, and in a modest career as a public servant presented so reasonable a view of the limitations as well as of the opportunities of American life that the testimony offered a completely acceptable indorsement of democracy. Allen's *Only Yesterday* (1931), a shrewd, amiable appraisal of the decade just past, indicated that America was capable of profiting by an unexcited re-examination of its mistakes. Constance Rourke, regarding American humor as a key to the sly but not sedulously kept secret of American character, made a revealing excursion into the country of the mind. *American Humor: A Study of the National Character* (1931) was far more successful than most such journeys of rediscovery because it was at all times under the discipline of a superior intelligence.

By this time serious writers no longer felt that they were obliged as critical men to believe, with Mencken, that the climate of American life was inevitably blighting to fine impulse or to elevated intention. Mark Twain, who had sat for Van Wyck Brooks for his portrait as a frustrated American, sat for another in 1932, and from this later canvas quite a different image emerged. The background was far less blighted, too. Bernard De Voto, having had access to new material, found that *Mark Twain's America* had not been the stultifying place it had been supposed to be. People lived spaciously, even graciously, on the frontier, and it was no sense of secret sin that had caused Mark Twain's melancholy. De Voto, who cannot read any positive statement without feeling a boyish desire to challenge it, was determined to reverse previous judgments. Making all necessary allowance for the chronic contentiousness of the writer, however, his picture of the times seemed as plausible as it was pleasant. American democracy received a kind of tacit indorsement from this testimony that the frontier had not been the rim of doom but a place of sunlit warmth and casual friendliness.

A figure of the times who embodied its spirit was Herbert Agar, who had begun his writing career as a poet and newspaper critic of poetry, but who had moved, through identification with the Southern agrarian group (which had published *I'll Take My Stand* in 1930), toward a deeper and deeper preoccupation with political, economic, and historical themes. In 1933 he published *The People's Choice,* a study of the workings of democracy intended to offer the warning that demagogues may steal leadership to which they have no right if the electorate proves to be momentarily indolent and unwatchful. Agar's finely disciplined style, touched with the ardor of profound conviction, has helped to make his intense earnestness acceptable even to readers who are ordinarily earnest about nothing but their wish to elude earnestness.

In the same year the journalistic prophets began to warn of the coming crisis in Europe. Hamilton Fish Armstrong's study *Hitler's Reich: The First Phase* pointed out that America no longer had any choice but to live in the great world, and that in a democracy where the people create their own programs a knowledge of foreign policy is a prerequisite of responsible citizenship.

By way of relaxation, the journalistic writers remembered

the lighter moods of the American past. Floyd Dell, a liberal whom the rise of communism had driven away from the causes to which he had previously been committed, had nothing to say of his political activities when he published the autobiographical study *Homecoming: An Autobiography*. Instead, he preferred to concentrate on the tragicomedy of a sensitive boy's approach to maturity in an American town.

To his study in *Timber Line* of the rugged and ribald individualism of the old West, Gene Fowler imparted the qualities of the tough-tender school of literature made popular by certain novelists. Later, in *Good Night, Sweet Prince*, a biographical study of the actor John Barrymore, extravagance and tastelessness took full possession of Fowler's gift. A kind of gaudy sentimentality began to show through his surface concern with riot and mayhem in the lives of the uninhibited.

During the middle 1930's, as the depression reached its climax, the journalistic writers became more concerned than ever with the rediscovery of the true character of native life. Out of that preoccupation there developed a new literary tradition to which the name "regionalism" was applied. The first studies that can be assigned definitely to this classification were books like those of Lyle Saxon in his interpretations of his city and his state.

Regionalism, still too new a term to be included in dictionaries that appeared in the late 1940's, has come, in the decade and a half that it has been in general use, to mean many things to many writers. Novelists, dramatists, and poets have become identified with it in the effort to find particularizing customs, tricks of speech, patterns of humor, and ethical concepts that can help to give universal passion a local habitation. Already regionalism has attracted to its practice, the exact limits of which are perhaps never to be defined, many who feel that theirs is a high religious calling. There is a tendency to encourage schisms within the cult, and each new group insists that the true faith is its exclusive possession. But the unifying purpose of the regionalists is simply to expose to view the full diversity of American life as particular conditions have tended to give lively variations to the patterns of thought and behavior within American borders.

A typical early product was Carl Carmer's *Stars Fell on Alabama* (1934), a cool, humorous, and sympathetic account of the Southern way of life. Scouting chiefly for ideas and attitudes that clarify a people's outlook on their experience, Carmer gathered up incidentally a rich supply of folklore. The immediate success of his book created a new career for Carmer, and, two years later, he published a similar reconstruction of the temper of upstate New York. *Listen for a Lonesome Drum* caught the rhythm and the ring of native legend and revealed the faith and fire at the heart of legend.

It was time, too, for the story of the new American to be told as he made his pilgrimage in reverse to recapture the heritage of his homeland. In 1934, Louis Adamic published *The Native's Return,* an account of his return as a man to the village in Yugoslavia he had left as a body of fifteen. The significance of the book lay in the fresh, candid, still boyish conviction of the author that today the only really good citizen is a citizen of the world. The older type of immigrant had come to America eager to forget the past; even when he faced the disheartening discovery that at least parts of the American dream were very far from fulfillment, he still rejected the closed culture of the old in favor of the openness of the new. Louis Adamic presented himself as the embodiment of the idea that even for the man who changes worlds, the idea of culture must be continuous; he must help to make a blend of what is valuable in the old with what is valuable in the new. Adamic's sound intuition made him one of the best internationalists among American writers.

Characteristic of the desire to rise above sectionalism or provincialism in American culture was Douglas Southall Freeman's four-volume biography of Robert E. Lee. Writing in odd moments snatched from the busy life of a newspaper editor, Freeman put together a vast amount of carefully assorted detail and created a study that is at once monumental and intimate. Lee, the military genius, the patriot of immaculate sentiment, is returned to American tradition not as a rebel but as a hero in whom to take pride.

Marquis James, in his two-volume biography of Andrew Jackson, proved that the serious journalist had also learned to resist the inclination to be a debunker. Seven years of sober study went into this new evaluation of a complex and highly controversial figure. Jackson, a soldier, a patriot, a friend, and a lover, offered many temptations to the biographer who would distort for the sake of sensationalism, but James neither sentimentalized nor caricatured Jackson.

Among autobiographical works of the period, none was more interesting as cultural history than Malcolm Cowley's *Exile's Return: A Narrative of Ideas* (1934; revised in 1951). Here the native American, a young man out of Pennsylvania and Harvard, was shown in his effort to come to terms with what European cultural forms, especially in their more recent manifestations, could offer him. With an openness of mind and an abundance of good will, Cowley diagnosed the fever of the Jazz Age and appraised the dominant figures among American expatriates in Paris. The emotion of those days was recollected in detached tranquillity rather than in the mood of hatred, regret, or uncertainty with which other men have rejected a past faith. Cowley's well-balanced, generous-minded account of the episode made it meaningful as part of America's effort to rediscover its true identity.

The year 1935 was significant for the journalists as the one in which many a reporter undertook to play the prophet's role. Foreign correspondents for American newspapers seemed to become aware all at once that they had a duty to make America conscious of its proper place in world affairs. Vincent Sheean's *Personal History*, destined to be recognized as the archetype of all the books which took as their theme the education of the American as internationalist, remains the best.

Another product of Chicago and of the *Chicago Daily News* foreign news bureau was James Negley Farson, who, in *The Way of a Transgressor,* managed to be simultaneously a prophet of internationalism and an exploiter of a private aptitude for mischief-making.

Anna Louise Strong spent many years edging her way into the collectivist philosophy and finally, in 1930, surrendered her mind to the communist idea. She created the first English newspaper in Russia, the Moscow *Daily News*. In *I Change Worlds: The Remaking of an American,* she wrote with a tremulous ardor about her new faith. Agnes Smedley, writing throughout the 1930's about the Chinese Communists, shared this ardor. Such books as *Chinese Destinies* (1933) and *China Fights Back* (1938) are dominated by a sense of desperate earnestness.

While America zigzagged slowly out of its isolationist position and many writers were obsessed with the immediate construction of a new system of politics, one highly gifted interpreter held close to the view that only the intimacies of our own deep, unchanging tradition could represent us truly. If it was important that America should find its way back into international society, it was no less important that it should understand its essential character as well as Clarence Day was able to help his fellow citizens to do.

Life with Father (1935) started fifteen years of pleasant drawing-room chatter about family relationships, in the course of which the journalistic gossips have said a great deal that was revealing and a great deal more that was merely facetious and trivial. But Clarence Day's own book offered a study of the American individualist in all the awe-inspiring impregnability of his integrity; it remains extremely valuable among works of analysis either more or less pretentious. The fact that the ethical position taken by this father and assumed to be unshakable was regularly circumvented by the discreet maneuvering of a mother who was less doctrinaire in philosophy but more humane in behavior, completed ideally the picture of democracy at work in the home. Few of Day's fellow writers were able to treat the democratic spirit in such intimate, domestic terms or in so easy a manner.

Missionary zeal possessed the serious journalists ever more intensely as the decade darkened under the war shadow. In 1936 their impulse to drive their fellow countrymen toward decision declared itself in a variety of earnest discussions. This was the year of John Gunther's *Inside Europe,* the most discursive, if far from being the most discerning, of the studies of dictatorship. Fully awakened at last to the crisis as it affected their own future, American readers absorbed Gunther's glib generalizations with the gratitude of amateur adventurers feeling an acute need of an intellectual Baedeker. In his *Sweden: The Middle Way,* Marquis Childs invited Americans to look scrutinizingly at a European experiment that offered a vivid contrast in aim to that of dictatorship. Granville Hicks, whose book *The Great Tradition* had offered a Marxist interpretation of American literature since the Civil War, continued in his *John Reed; The Making of a Revolutionary* to expound the rebel spirit.

Two American scholars who were also journalists examined the diversity and the contrasts of American life in the autobiography clinic. Henry Seidel Canby was cool, detached, critical, and just as he subjected education in New England to sober review in *Alma Mater: The Gothic Age of the American College.* Carl Van Doren, in *Three Worlds,* traced the pilgrimage of a thoroughly normal American from the days of boyhood as a football enthusiast in an Illinois town, through the later quiet adventures of a scholar and teacher, and on, finally, to the strenuous concerns of an editor and impresario of the book world. Van Doren's story, like his presence, had the virtue of seeming to reflect a reassuring strength and solidity; for once, more of simple forthrightness than of flair for audacity characterized the confessions of a bookman.

An ambitious gatherer and reclaimer of every item of the native tradition was Constance Lindsay Skinner, who launched under her editorship a series of American studies. It was her idea that our native civilization might well be examined as it moved westward along the inland water routes of the country. She undertook to stimulate writers with fresh insights to approach the problems of history, retaining unapologetically their interests as poets, novelists, and folklorists in the homely drama of daily life. The *Rivers of America* series was inaugurated in 1937 with *Kennebec: Cradle of Americans,* in which the semi-official poet of Maine, Robert P. T. Coffin, paid lyrical tribute to the life of that region; and with *Upper Mississippi: A Wilderness Saga,* a celebration by Walter Havighurst of the contribution made to American culture by the most easily assimilated of its immigrants, the Scandinavians. At the rate of two or three volumes a year, the collection grew; Blair Niles added *The James;* Carl Carmer greatly enriched its distinction with *The Hudson;* Henry Seidel Canby contributed *The Brandywine;* Clyde Brion Davis, *The Arkansas;* and, in collaboration with A. J. Hanna, James Branch Cabell, *The St. Johns.* Varying greatly in the quality of its individual studies, the series as a whole, under the later editorship of Stephen Vincent Benét, Carl Carmer, and Hervey Allen, achieved its purpose, which was to serve as a storehouse of American lore.

The world was moving toward war on a global basis, and American journalists returned from all the barricades with news of the crisis. Even when these examinations were not well balanced they were earnest, detailed, factual. Eugene Lyons in *Assignment in Utopia* (1937) told, with a shocked intensity that sometimes seemed naïve, the story of his disillusionment with Soviet Russia. Edgar Snow in *Red Star Over China* (1937) raised the curtain on one of the dramas of the century, about which Americans had previously known almost nothing. In his *The Life and Death of a Spanish Town* (1937), Elliot Paul forgot, temporarily, the more raucous of his many curious talents in order to write with deeply moving sympathy of the misery and the magnificence of Franco's victims. Paul's acute sense of identification with the sufferings of a simple people engaged in a losing struggle for freedom touched the American consciousness intimately. This was an unmistakable sign that, in the process of reaching a closer comprehension of its own values, America had achieved a sharper awareness of the world community, of its needs and its rights.

It was now as part of the world community that America saw itself. In 1938, Louis Adamic published *My America, 1928–1938,* in which he urged with renewed eloquence that the heritages of all peoples be blended into the world culture that America seemed destined to found and to develop. Even some of the Marxist critics of our political democracy wished to assert their faith in the ability of the native tradition to adapt itself to changing traditions, as did Granville Hicks in *I Like America*. Austere Yankee morality, chastening what it loved, characterized Hicks's idealism. Carl Van Doren found, in his biography of Benjamin Franklin, that the native genius which his subject embodied was composed of common sense, adaptability, the experimental temper, and the co-operative spirit, exactly as it is embodied in the best of contemporary leaders.

The journalistic prophets worked with the zeal of self-imposed responsibility to implant in American minds serious values with regard to world society. Max Lerner, with the sedate aggressiveness that has always characterized his editorial style, warned that in the world crisis *It is Later Than You Think*. Louis Fischer, lately disabused of an earlier enchantment with the Soviet experiment, urged in *Men and Politics* a sober reconsideration of what America's role must be in the inevitable reordering of the world.

The 1930's came to an end with the most vigorous statement yet recorded of the principles developed out of the bitter conflicts of the day. Samuel Hopkins Adams and Oswald Garrison Villard, elders among liberal journalists, who were alike only in their devotion to idealism, offered charteristic utterances. In the *Incredible Era: The Life and*

Times of Warren Gamaliel Harding (1939), Adams showed that he had lost neither the zeal that had marked his muckraking activities nor the verve that had made him a popular entertainer among novelists. He exposed the shabby frauds of the last mass assault on public virtue in Washington with a thoroughness that left no poker party unvisited and no mysterious loot bags unopened. Villard, soon to end his career as a conspicuous crusading editor, offered in *Fighting Years: Memoirs of a Liberal Editor* (1939) an account of his stewardship as the inheritor of a long tradition of devotion to causes; like his grandfather and his father he had been an indefatigable defender of the great tradition of liberty.

Edna Ferber, another journalist who had turned successfully to fiction, did American tradition the honor of submitting it to sharp criticism in her autobiography *A Peculiar Treasure*. Her childhood sufferings from anti-Semitism in a small Midwestern town opened a vigorous drama that ended in a personal triumph over bigotry. Edna Ferber's training as a novelist necessarily helped her to dramatize the story, but the depth of her feeling about this plague of the human spirit raised her autobiography to a level high above that of her thin, meretricious fiction.

The young crusaders among the foreign correspondents brought their records down to date in 1939 as the dictators abandoned all pretense to peaceful intention. Vincent Sheean, who had put himself honorably in the forefront of the fight to awaken the world to its danger, added a grim final word before the battle in *Not Peace but A Sword*. Pierre van Paassen continued to fight the dictatorships which, one after another, had closed their borders to him. The strong religious and ethical feelings that crowded the lines of his factual accounts made *Days of Our Years* seem like a completely fulfilled and ennobled recapitulation of all the themes that the journalist as prophet had been announcing throughout the decade.

The entertainments provided by men and women who could turn momentarily away from the international scene were characteristic of the decade. Bellamy Partridge and Ruth McKenney enrolled themselves as followers of the Clarence Day school of investigation. Partridge in *Country Lawyer* helped himself to the design of *Life with Father,* but he did not enrich his tribute to eccentricity with much in the way of distinction. Ruth McKenney was prompted by Day's success to examine her own experience, and she did so with gratifying freshness. *My Sister Eileen* dramatized the awe, the apprehension, and the amusement with which a clever sister watches the inevitable entanglements in the life of a beautiful sister; so engaging was the honest gaiety of this performance that the literature of comedy was enriched with one more generously and graciously observed item.

v

The depression, which has done so much throughout the 1930's to change American minds, affected them in still another significant way when the writers' projects were organized by the federal government. Men and women of creative and interpretive talent, rescued from humiliation and want, set to work on a series of state guides. Directors of superior ability—Harlan Hatcher in Ohio, for example, and Lyle Saxon in Louisiana—steered these efforts so successfully that the volumes produced under this co-operative enterprise were recognized as having distinct and permanent value. Another storehouse of American lore had been provided.

Throughout the 1940's editors and publishers sought new and beguiling ways of presenting the drama of American life as personal experience. The impulse of regionalism flowered and spread through one series after another: the Sovereign States group, the Seaport Cities, the Folkways, the Highways. To these collections belong *The Buckeye Country: A Pageant of Ohio* by Harlan Hatcher, *Lake Superior* by Grace Lee Nute, *Lake Champlain and Lake George* by Frederic F. Van de Water, *Our Southwest* by Erna Fergusson, *Northwest Gateway: The Story of the Port of Seattle* by Archie Binns, *Desert Country* by Edwin Corle, *Deep Delta Country* by Harnett Kane, *Mormon Country* by Wallace Stegner, *Short Grass Country* by Stanley Vestal (Walter Campbell), *Southern California Country* by Carey McWilliams, *The National Road* by Philip Jordan. The *Rivers* series continued as Donald Davidson brought the Tennessee into the mighty confluence.

The impulse to bring into clear focus various aspects of the American compulsion toward its destiny produced entirely new techniques for the study of history. Bernard De Voto's *The Year of Decision: 1841* offers an example. Here the records of pre-Civil War expeditions, the purpose of which was to possess the West, are presented as a complete account of the expansionist movement; the activities of Frémont, of the Mountain Men, of the Donner party fall into place as related parts of a great pageant. De Voto's later book *Across the Wide Missouri* developed the theme further with particular emphasis upon the Mountain Men.

In the year of Pearl Harbor the voice of the journalist, speaking as prophet, was raised louder than ever. Indeed the prophets' chorus swelled so mightily as to drown out all competition. The theme was the inescapable duty of supporting democratic ideals. Louis Adamic's *Two Way Passage* said, in effect, that it is more blessed to give than to receive freedom and that this must be America's foreign policy. Herbert Agar, as editor of *The City of Democracy,* imparted to all his colleagues in the symposium the dedicated belief that the cause of world freedom must launch a new crusade. Max Lerner expanded the interpretation of values offered in *Ideas Are Weapons: The History and Uses of Ideas* in a study which he threateningly entitled *Ideas for the Ice Age;* only the warmth of world co-operation, he suggested, could avert freezing extinction for civilization.

In the last moment of suspense before America's entrance into world conflict, journalistic observers offered their final warnings. H. R. Knickerbocker seemed to impart the inflammatory character of his own red pigmentation of hair to the pages of his question-and-answer book *Is Tomorrow Hitler's?* John Gunther moved on in his methodical way *Inside Latin America.* His card-catalogue system of social interpretation recorded important aspects of the Latin affinity with dictatorship. Joseph C. Harsch, later to be one of the oracles of the air, offered a candid analysis of the purposes of dictatorship in *Pattern of Conquest.* Hanson Baldwin, the *New York Times* military editor, countered with the soothing suggestion, *United We Stand.* Eugene Lyons deliberately goaded his readers into fresh alarm over the threat of communism with a report menacingly entitled *The Red Decade.* Edward R. Murrow transferred to paper, in *This Is London,* something of the highly dramatic quality of his trans-Atlantic broadcasts, communicating to America an awareness of the stoically endured sufferings of the British people under the blitz. William Shirer's *Berlin Diary: The Journal of a Foreign*

Correspondent, a hardly less stoical account of a journalist's daily martyrdom under Nazi arrogance, presented stunning evidence of how degrading it is to make a political program of the basest kinds of bigotry and ignorance. Leland Stowe, one of the most civilized and graceful of the journalistic prophets, supported the earnest pleas of all the others for co-operation among the democracies; his book *No Other Road to Freedom* put the basic issue clearly and emphatically before American readers. Perhaps no more honorable record of foresight—high-minded and, for the most part, unhysterical—exists in the history of journalism than that represented by the work of American observers in the last hour before Pearl Harbor. They may be credited with a large share in the indoctrination of the American as a world citizen.

Writers who are addicted to the production of what journalists call "think pieces" engaged in a long debate about theoretical values. Theodore Dreiser, clinging to his leftist sympathies, argued in 1941 that *America Is Worth Saving* (according, of course, to his own formula), while Henry Luce observed that this is *The American Century.* Occupying the middle ground, Ralph Ingersoll insisted that *America Is Worth Fighting For.* Gerald Johnson, one of the ablest of the oncoming journalistic interpreters, put before the public an inevitable question of the time, *Roosevelt: Dictator or Democrat?,* and answered it with an emphatic indorsement of American leadership. At no time in American history had the issues of major political and social problems been expounded so fully and freely; never had interpreters had so much success in moving a people away from the spirit of isolationism toward an acceptance of responsibility in world leadership.

A meeting of native pride with this intensified sense of

duty characterized the spirit of many new and fresh interpretations of the past. Dixon Wecter's *The Hero in America*
offered a scholar's close examination of the values that constituted the philosophy of American leadership. Carl Van
Doren's *Secret History of the American Revolution,* utiliz-
ing a mass of newly discovered material, was similarly concerned with the problem of putting order to a pattern of
democratic belief.

In a more audacious and exuberant fashion Harnett Kane
in *Louisiana Hayride: The American Rehearsal for Dictatorship, 1928–1940* called the Huey Long machine to account for its sins against the democratic tradition. If Harnett Kane raised his voice loud in protest he did so in the
hope of drowning out the voices of demagogues who were
still making their raucous appeals to ignorance.

Jonathan Daniels published in 1941 the third of a series
of good-tempered and discerning interpretations of contemporary American character. The importance of *A Southerner Discovers the South, A Southerner Discovers New England,* and *Tar Heels: A Portrait of North Carolina* lies in
the fact that each turns the steady light of insight into the
dark corners of the continuing hostility between the North
and the South.

The journalists who had traveled far from their editorial
desks sometimes brought their experiences together for examination in the form of autobiography. Josephus Daniels's
two-volume autobiography *An Editor in Politics* presented
a particularly dramatic account of the experiences of a man
who managed to be simultaneously a Southerner and a puritan, a politician and a reformer, a journalist and a man of
letters. Irvin S. Cobb in *Exit Laughing* invited inspection
of a temperament no less rich and varied, that of a popular
entertainer who was at the same time a shrewd interpreter of

native character. And Thomas Ybarra in *Young Man of Caracas* looked back through a nostalgic light at the pleasant glitter of his youth in South America.

In 1944, just before his death, Wendell Willkie published the book *One World,* which announced the theme that was to capture and hold the attention of many a serious journalist during the rest of the decade. In it a lawyer turned business executive, turned politician, turned interpreter of social problems, put before the large public of his admirers his lately discovered, hastily recorded conviction that only co-operation among all the nations of the world could enable the human family to survive comfortably and in dignity.

vi

The books that crowded onto the shelves after World War II (crowding out of mind the flurried accounts of war experience with which the publishing world had been largely concerned during the struggle) offered many variations of this theme. By 1946 writers had become preoccupied with the problem of Russia; but men who had insisted before on the need to beware of the philosophy of Soviet leaders now tried once more to encourage the co-operative temper. In *The Great Challenge,* Louis Fischer, an outspoken critic of Russia, urged upon America the wisdom of organizing for mutual protection the three-fourths of the world that was already committed to the democratic ideal. The door must not be closed on Russia, Fischer insisted, but the countries under her domination must be made to understand the power that reposed in the unified effort of the rest of the world. While diplomats like William Bullitt (in *The Great Globe Itself*) and Sumner Welles (in *Where Are We*

Heading?) raised their questions, journalists continued to fill the roles of prophets. Eric Sevareid insisted stubbornly that it was *Not So Wild A Dream* to believe that all men everywhere could be persuaded at last to accept the idea of their inescapable interdependence. E. B. White in *The Wild Flag* combined the shrewdness of a Yankee observer with the literary refinement of a Chinese philosopher in a survey of the outlook for world peace. He put the most challenging of all questions: Why not?

In *Thunder Out of China,* Theodore H. White and Annalee Jacoby stubbornly insisted that adjustments would not be easy in a world where leaders were still inclined to talk democracy while they practiced ruthless dictatorship.

Related to the eagerness of the political journalists to urge upon their countrymen a sober and inquiring attitude toward human affairs was the impulse, strikingly evident in the 1940's, of another group of interpreters who would force Americans to look intimately at every aspect of the problem of man's inhumanity toward man. Enclosed in journalist John Hersey's unsensational yet moving account of what had happened at *Hiroshima* was the implication that, if the dropping of the bomb could be considered necessary in order to end the struggle quickly, still the cruel suffering that it imposed on men, women, and children remained part of a grim and dismal record of human failure. The memory of that guilt could be eased only by a conscientious effort to make sure that no such struggle could occur again. On the edge of the journalistic world stood such lively figures as Margaret Halsey, making similar appeals to the justice of the heart in the solution of social problems. In *Color Blind,* Miss Halsey oddly but attractively matched a strong ethical sense with a piquant wit in an effort to cover every possible approach to the problem of racial discrimination.

The searching of the past went on as vigorously as an ever

increasing number of serious journalists undertook to describe the American scene. In *Land of the Dacotahs*, Bruce
Nelson had a distinguished success in showing how the wild
beauty of a place had helped to form the character and the
outlook of the human beings who enacted the drama of
their lives against its background. In *Lost Men of American
History*, Stewart Holbrook briskly rescued from the foot-
notes some shapers of American destiny who deserved not
to be forgotten. In *Frontier on the Potomac*, Jonathan Daniels related past to present and present to probable future
in a shrewd study of the essential qualities of American
leadership.

In the late years of the 1940's the academic interpreters
were ready at last to attempt a complete formulation of an
answer to Charles Eliot's question: What is an American?
The Shaping of the American Tradition (1947) offered
Louis M. Hacker's survey of the country of the American
mind. To excerpts from the significant documents of American history the editor put his revealing introductory comments. America, Hacker found to be a world of its citizens'
own making; a new kind of economic leadership had been
raised up out of its own universal middle class; its unique
governmental design of limited, controlled, and balanced
authorities had managed to keep the popular will supreme.

Once more the journalists went to work to offer further
documentation. Hacker's view of the uniqueness of the
American tradition was supported by analyses of the popular will like John Gunther's *Inside U.S.A.*, the last of the
author's hyperthyroid drives toward gathering up all the
facts of social intercourse that strew the surface of the globe.
One of the best-known journalistic seers sat for his portrait
against the background of his Kansas community in Walter
Johnson's discerning, critical, sympathetic study *William
Allen White's America*.

The year 1948 marked a new coming-of-age among American writers as interpreters of the experience of a people engaged in making a new world. In *The Age of the Great Depression,* Dixon Wecter was able to show how a bold revolution had been worked quietly but confidently in our society. A time that might well have been one of demoralization had proved rather to be one in which more serviceable patterns of democracy had been achieved; once more the system of balanced authorities had kept the popular will supreme— and healthy. In *The Great Rehearsal,* Carl Van Doren showed the experimental spirit of democracy at work under the discipline of the co-operative temper as, after the American Revolution, the colonies put off all their hostilities and mutual suspicions to achieve unity at last. This experience, Van Doren suggested, might well make America the needed leader in a co-operative enterprise looking toward world government.

Internal problems of adjustment were considered on a high level of seriousness by Carey McWilliams in *A Mask for Privilege: Anti-Semitism in America* and by W. L. White in *Lost Boundaries.* The first book dismissed all the easy explanations of anti-Semitism and found a subtly poisonous and persuasive influence toward bigotry in the desire of a self-appointed ruling class to protect its position; just as Hitler offered his followers a formula for hatred to blind them into docile discipleship, so a type of American leader had done the same. The second book showed the first fissures appearing in the wall between Negroes and white men, with each group looking wistfully, distrustfully, yet hopefully through at the other.

The career of the American humorist during the first half of the twentieth century has been creditably marked by the quiet determination of a group of high-spirited men and women to keep individuality alive in a time of chilling conformity to the obvious formulas of wit. The tendency of the mass forms of entertainment—the screen, the radio, television—to standardize the joke and to popularize the machine-made gag has been opposed resolutely by writers who have taken the oblique view of human experience and transformed its vagaries into surprising and delightful art forms. It may even be said that contemporary writers have been responsible for the redesigning of humor in a greater variety of styles than it had previously shown. The tall story, regarded once as the specialty of the native artist, has tended to disappear and to be replaced by a gratifyingly irresponsible company of jokes, most of them slight, sly, and sometimes a little sad.

The newspaper columnists searched through this realm with the quiet zeal of collectors of rare objects. Bert Leston Taylor, who died in 1921, had set a new fashion in his editorial-page feature of the *Chicago Tribune* called "A Line-o'-Type or Two." Urbane, civilized, a little aloof, Taylor delighted his readers by pointing out the absurdities of American social life. A reference in a small town paper to a "quiet wedding" brought from him the comment: "Unmarred by the usual screams of the bridegroom." His disciple Franklin P. Adams began his career in Chicago on the *Journal* and carried it to its finest point when "The Conning Tower" appeared in the New York *World* during the 1920's, offering a most attractive glimpse into the humane studies of a studio habitué. Adams was a gourmet of gossip; his reliable taste created a new standard for the columnist-critic. Another Chicago columnist Keith Preston contributed to the *Daily News* witty translations from Horace. Don Marquis of the New York *Sun* enriched American folklore with many creatures of his gently satiric fancy, including the Greenwich Village aesthete Hermione surrounded by her "little group of serious thinkers" and Archy, the "educated cockroach," whose contributions to the wealth of native humor are invaluable.

Two magazines, *Vanity Fair* and *Life* (predecessor of the present picture publication), developed writers whose small but steady candles of inspiration illuminated many alcoves of American society. Robert Benchley's reputation as a wit rests on his unobtrusive and genial flair for ineptitude. His famous *Treasurer's Report and Other Aspects of Community Singing* offers an example. He also had a fine approach to dramatic criticism, and from his attack no sins of silliness were hidden. In a clumsily fabricated melodrama which he once reviewed, a character addicted to pidgin English introduced herself, as she appeared out of a tropical storm, saying: "Me Nubi. Me good girl. Me stay." Benchley commented: "Me Benchley. Me bad boy. Me go." Dorothy Parker, despite a talent of a limited sort, managed, in her time as a magazine writer, to become a living legend as an audacious wit. To the stories and verse that made her the most quoted of women (Sappho and Mme de Sévigné included) she has added criticism of a gleaming malice unmatched by any of her colleagues. Robert Sherwood prefaced his long and useful career as a dramatist by producing for *Life* and *Vanity Fair* the first readable criticisms of motion pictures.

The creation in 1925 of *The New Yorker* provided a secure shelter for many new writers with a talent for picking up, with the precision of radar, the faraway echoes of human frailty. E. B. White was perhaps the most fastidiously discerning of these men and women, but James Thurber, with whom White collaborated on *Is Sex Necessary?* (1929), has been able to weave the cobweb of his wit over a wider variety of interests always with completely reliable taste. *My Life and Hard Times* (1933) admitted Thurber to the Clarence Day school for the examination of zany relatives. Other books, *Let Your Mind Alone* (1937), *The Last Flower* (1939), and *The White Deer* (1945) opened many magic casements. Thurber would be unclassifiable even if he had not taken to complicating the problem further with his weird and disturbing drawings of "the war of men and women." The integrity of a highly personal gift has seldom been guarded so scrupulously or remained so delicately surprising.

Alexander Woollcott, through many essays like those gathered together in the volume *While Rome Burns* (1934), achieved a wide audience as *chroniqueur de scandale*. The glint of his affected style attracted the eyes of even sedate readers and drew their sympathetic attention to his critical enthusiasms for the second- and third-rate works of English and American art.

As book reviewer for *The New Yorker* during a long period, Clifton Fadiman treated literature as though it were a great public fair. The well-modulated and enticing tones of his voice as a barker for books brought many to his booth. *Reading I've Liked* (1941), an anthology, preserves some of his typical literary comments.

Ogden Nash's gift for creating utter confusion out of the traditions of didactic verse has brought him to all sorts of improper and heart-warming conclusions about duty, parenthood, and ambition. His outsize couplets and their tormented rhymes have become world-famous. *The Bad Parents' Garden of Verse* (1936) and *I'm a Stranger Here Myself* (1938) contain his wittiest assaults on stuffiness.

Arthur Kober has explored the native customs of the

Bronx as though it were a foreign realm in which a different language was spoken. *Thunder Over the Bronx* (1935), *Having Wonderful Time* (1937), and *My Dear Bella* (1941) are sly analogues of anthropological treatises. S. J. Perelman, whose distaste for the pretentious and the false has made him the adroit enemy of the literary traditions of snob advertising and of the best-selling novel, has recorded his protests in *Dawn Ginbergh's Revenge* (1929) and *Keep It Crisp* (1946). His air of patient wonder in the face of the monstrous has made him a unique critic of American mores. Leo Rosten's *The Education of H*Y*M*A*N K*A*P*L*A*N* found a notable hero of American comedy in the ranks of the earnest, amiable, wildly confused students in Americanization classes. Frank Sullivan, whose cliché expert Mr. Arbuthnot may have helped to cure writers of the habit of beating dead phrases, has devoted two decades to the tireless pursuit of absurdity in *The Life and Times of Martha Hepplethwaite* (1926) and, still in a mood of gamin restlessness, in *A Rock in Every Snowball* (1946).

The political commentators have availed themselves fully of the democratic privilege of free expression to fly every kind of banner that their temperamental traits have prompted them to catch up. Heywood Broun, whose sponsorship of the liberal point of view had the pages, first, of the New York *World* and, later, of *The New Republic* as forum, wrote always with the relaxed joviality of a man who had just stepped from the poker table. His sincerity in the defense of causes, like that of Sacco and Vanzetti, was not the less touching or persuasive for its being expressed in the idiom of the average man rather than in that of the nimbus-wearing prophet. Heywood Broun, like many another newspaper interpreter of the social scene, had come into the realm of ideas by way of the sports desk and the drama desk. Earlier enthusiasms did not desert him as later ones were added, and the quality of spontaneous delight in human experience as sport always gave him a light step when he moved as the crusader.

Certain journalists at the end of the half century, like others at its beginning, clung to the right to demonstrate love of democracy by vituperative attacks on what they took to be its flaws. Westbrook Pegler, another sports-writer-turned-thinker, directed the fire of his inexhaustible store of hatred against all those with whose political ideas he disagreed. His newspaper columns, gathered together in such volumes as *The Dissenting Opinions of Mr. Westbrook Pegler* (1938), scorched many reputations, but they did little serious damage. Dorothy Thompson has retained a kind of maternal fervor in all her admonitions to the American public about domestic affairs and foreign policy. Her talents—quick absorption of other people's ideas, brisk decision and undeflectability in support of a decision once taken, disciplinary firmness in the face of a stubborn opponent—all these are feminine talents, and Dorothy Thompson has represented industriously and conscientiously the *Hausfrau* trying to tidy up the slovenly world. Taking home and mother (or Mom) as his theme, Philip Wylie in *Generation of Vipers* (1942) preached a kind of "anti-sermon." His histrionic recklessness was no less marked than was Pegler's. The two raged furiously but, in their extravagance, they seemed like reversions to literary types of an earlier day when journalism had been personal to the point of being scandalous and exuberant to the point of hysteria.

The *Saturday Review of Literature,* established in 1924 as an entity separate from its parent publication, the *New York Post,* developed a group of writing men who exercised a pervasive influence on taste and opinion. Christopher Morley, more widely known for his novels, pleased a devoted audience with his column of literary comment, "The Bowling Green." In it he found room to record the casual romances of a bibliophile and the more rugged adventures of a wanton with words whose passion for puns, coinages, and tricks of phrase was inexhaustible. As many of these little raids on the sedate strongholds of the language were translated into printed form, Morley, active as a contributing editor of the *Saturday Review* until 1940, revealed himself ever more clearly as a puckish semischolar with a zeal for keeping the values of literature alive and keeping them lively. William Rose Benét in "The Phoenix Nest," another department of the same journal, conducted literary conversations with his correspondents, and these tended, as Benét approached the end of his life, to become more and more concerned with the principles of human fellowship in world society. Norman Cousins, in a later phase, used his editorial post as one from which to explore the ideas with which so many writing men had become concerned, those of the cause of internationalism. His *Modern Man Is Obsolete* (1945) was characteristic of his urgent style in recommending the discipline of world government as the only hope for the security of civilization. John Mason Brown, having established himself with a large following as a kind of unofficial American *arbiter elegantiarum* of plays, films, and books, broadened the interests of his department "Seeing Things" to include these social and political values as they declared themselves in the writing of the time.

It was this tendency to seize upon the broader responsibility of the interpreter that characterized the development of the journalist as literary man during the first half of the twentieth century. Like his predecessor he was concerned with expounding the doctrine of the continuing advance of democracy toward the fulfillment of an ideal society of free men. Unlike his predecessor he was not content to take the parochial view of his task.

In editorial, column, interpretive essay, the journalist of the 1850's had been a vehement celebrant of local pride, a militant defender of the local issue. The realm that he took as his own was small; the interest that he displayed in its advancement was enormous. He spoke with the brassy, repetitive enthusiasm of the circus barker, and in his use of language his art seemed to be on the level of that of a steam calliope.

The writing of the contemporary journalist is quite different. The interests of America have become many, and the undaunted newspaper writer has undertaken boldly to interpret them all. As the nature of the state has changed, as population centers have shifted, as science and industrialization have modified our way of life, as the values of religious life and family life have lost the character they had in the nineteenth century's afterglow of puritanism, the journalist has looked at the vast, variegated, and confused scene that is American life. Inevitably, he has written about it in his own way, employing his own inflections, and he has stressed the one theme which his professional interests keep in the fore part of his consciousness: the discovery of America.

3

AMERICAN SOCIAL THOUGHT IN THE TWENTIETH CENTURY

WALTER METZGER

For all its rich complexity, American social thought in recent times dwells upon an age-old problem—the problem of *diversity* versus *solidarity*. Wherever he appears, the diversitarian says: "Focus on the individual! Enlarge his range of free choices; protect his life, his liberty, his property; accept his ethnic and intellectual differences!" "Focus on society!" the solidarist always entreats. "Plan for a rational and secure existence; safeguard the nation; minimize differences for the good of the whole!" America pledged herself to diversity in her rustic and revolutionary youth, and held to that pledge in her industrial coming-of-age. The twentieth century—with its social crises and its solidaristic drifts—challenged this traditional commitment.

More critically than ever before, American social theorists were compelled to re-evaluate the inherited faith, to redefine the diversity-solidarity issue, and, depending on the pressure of events, to offer new approaches and solutions.

i—THE CULT OF ECONOMIC INDIVIDUALISM

The American of around the mid-nineteenth century expected enormous benefits from a society in which each individual made his own economic decisions, unfettered by law or tradition. Not all of the benefits he expected were economic in the narrow sense. To be sure, he thought that widespread material well-being would follow, since each man best judged his own interest, and that interest was maximum gain. But he also assumed that character would be strengthened, since *laissez faire* was conducive to self-reliance, private property to the flowering of personality, work and thrift to moral improvement. Most important of all, he believed that through the automatic laws of the market capital would be accumulated, goods would be competitively improved, and wealth would be distributed justly among the various factors of production. He thought social harmony would evolve from intense individualistic competition—as though in a secular transubstantiation. Attracting native and immigrant, worker and owner, this millenial faith in economic individualism became the basis for a popular cult. Save for the ante-bellum lords of the South and some unhappy intellectuals, few dissented; paradoxically, this cult of diversity was a strong cohesive bond for the sprawling nation. Classical economics, political liberalism, and natural rights jurisprudence constituted its theology. Inevitable progress was its principle article of faith.

The first strong doubts appeared toward the close of the

century. The economy was then maturing; the frontier was filling up. Social rifts and tensions dimmed the bright early promise of harmony. There were a new wealthy elite and a new unemployed army; flourishing trusts and worsening depressions; class war at Homestead and Pullman. Even the faithful were demanding that the state restore harmony by fiat of free silver or the income tax, while, from outside the fold, the cohorts of Marx and Bellamy offered more drastic solidaristic solutions. This was the social setting in which the social Darwinists refurbished the argument for economic individualism, reconciling harmony and conflict, progress and poverty, with the dialectic of Herbert Spencer.

William Graham Sumner, the Yale economist-sociologist, was the most eminent spokesman for the cult in this period. In dozens of articles written in a popular and imperious style, Sumner expounded a rigid ethic of self-help. "A human being has a life to live, a career to run," wrote this Episcopal rector turned teacher. "He is a center of powers to work and capacities to suffer. What his powers may be—whether they carry him far or not; what his chances may be, whether wide or restricted; what his fortune may be, whether to suffer much or little—are questions which he must work out and endure as best he can."[1] Lest he preach Stoicism to the winds, Sumner propped his ethic with what he thought were the conclusions of modern science. Biological variation decreed that no two organisms be alike: in talent, strength or intelligence. To Sumner, diversity in nature indicated diversity in society. When each man makes his own way, natural selection becomes an unerring test of fitness, and the struggle for survival forces everyone to the test. What then if some fail and others succeed? This can only be on the basis of intrinsic ability and merit.

[1] *What Social Classes Owe to Each Other* (New York, Harper, 1883), p. 34.

What if failure is total for some and success inordinate for others? This merely proves that a higher civilization offers greater punishments and rewards. What if competition for success is intense? This ultimately leads to the improvement of the quality of the race. Thus, by a series of deductions Sumner converted evolution, a biological theory, into a sociological principle; the survival of the fittest, a tautology, into an empirical law; this empirical law, itself non-normative, into authority for the ethic of self-reliance. In defending the cult of economic individualism, Sumner declared that poverty and conflict were not evils but augurs of good, not end products of the social process but by-products. This was casuistry, but it had behind it the strength of a forceful personality and the supreme authority of science.

As Sumner understood science, it was a body of fixed laws, not a method for experiment and discovery. Gradually, as he shifted his interest from Mancunian economics to social evolutionism and social anthropology, he added proof to proof that social laws were immutable. In the manner of Burke, he emphasized the inertia of institutions and their historical continuity. In the manner of Malthus, he vetoed schemes to help the poor by referring to the ratio of men to land. In the manner of Spencer, he stressed the complexity of society, the "arbitrary, sentimental and artificial" results of legislative intermeddling. And in his last book—the famous *Folkways* (1907)—he held that society's mores were intractable, and that the masses, controlled by its mores, were in consequence hidebound and inert. Sumner's key idea—that men could comprehend social laws but not control them—was social determinism brought to a high finish. Tariffs, poor laws, private charity—all such expedients were wrong because they attempted to repeal the unrepealable, to alter the unalterable design. This rationale of inevitability carried the substance, but little of the spirit, of the inherited creed of diversity. When Sumner said *"laissez faire!"* it was less a call to creative action than a strident cry of futility.

In certain respects, this antiegalitarian, strenuous, deterministic version of economic individualism fitted the mood of the early 1900's. Its mordant realism went well with an age starting to outgrow its taste for the smiling aspects of life. Its accent on process and mechanistic laws was the accent, also, of a burgeoning machine culture. Its justification of struggle was in tune (Spencer's specific dissent notwithstanding) with imperialism and the bid for empire. And the economic autonomy it prescribed appealed to many Americans and continued to do so deep into the century, even after Middletown entered transition. Yet, at the same time, there were powerful social currents moving in an opposite direction. Sumner's "forgotten man" of the middle class, losing in the competitive race, was reluctant to accept the iron relation of worth to consequences. Critics of the Robber Barons attacked the doctrine of natural selection as a vendible form of the conservative rule—"What is, is right." And, not least, the suffering of *The Jungle* and *The Bitter Cry of the Children* awakened a strong humanitarian protest and a reaction against the brief that "God bade self-love and social be the same." Out of these ferments a new and significant approach to the diversity-solidarity problem emerged in the early part of the century.

ii—PROGRESSIVISM

"Progressivism" is a term ambiguously used to cover a political movement and a social philosophy. As a political movement it denotes a reform crusade in want of a consistent program. Under its banner men sought both to elect the militaristic Roosevelt and to write treaties of arbitration; to banish the trusts outright and to curb merely their excesses; to foster independent regulatory commissions and to make the government more responsive to the people. But, as a social philosophy, progressivism denotes a fairly consistent structure of ideas. Progressive education, functional psychology, the economic interpretation of history, sociological jurisprudence, institutional economics, pragmatism and instrumentalism were its dovetailing conceptions. John Dewey, Charles A. Beard, Oliver Wendell Holmes, Jr., and Thorstein Veblen were some of its great expositors.

Negatively, these leaders of progressivism tried to disentangle the concept of diversity from the imperative of *laissez faire,* the ethic of self-assertion, the whole emphasis on economic individualism. To do this, they attacked the theory of fixed laws: the social Darwinistic imprint in sociology, the concept of normality in economics, the formalistic approach to politics, history, and law. On the positive side, they reaffirmed certain fundamental notions of diversity: the value of the clash and play of diverse minds, and of creative self-expression. But every individual act, they held, is social in origin, public in nature, community-wide in effects. There is a single flow of human experience; the nineteenth century, with its false antithesis between the individual and the social, severed men from organic relations, starved the personality, created a rugged—and ragged—individualism. They were critical of the institutions that incorporated this fallacy, particularly of the institution of private ownership. But, Veblen excepted, they contemplated no violent or drastic change. They were intellectuals, with the intellectuals' emphasis on ideas, and they believed that the first site of social improvement was the mind and the imagination. They reckoned opinion more powerful than armies, educators more potent than generals; they hoped to unite scholarship and the concerns of life, the intelligentsia and the mass. Still moved by the saga of the nation's advance, they believed in human perfectibility and social improvement. Thus, if none of them believed with old David Hughes in the *World of Chance* that "the way to have the golden age is to elect it with the Australian ballot," neither did any believe—at least in this period—that man's sinfulness, stupidity, or fears would make the golden age difficult to recognize or impossible to achieve.

John Dewey built the philosophical scaffolding for progressivism. No other American thinker of the half century approached the Aristotelian inclusiveness with which Dewey related formal philosophy to social theory: to economics, history, politics, education, and psychology. For social theory, the last was of particular importance. This philosopher was no armchair theorist in the field of psychology. He worked under G. Stanley Hall at Johns Hopkins University in America's first psychological laboratory; cofounded the movement known as "functionalism"; developed (in conjunction with George H. Mead) certain basic concepts in social psychology; wrote an important commentary on the reflex-arc concept; applied his psychological theories to education. But the importance of his work far transcends the value of his purely technical contributions. His passionate conviction that human nature is pliant, impulsive, intelligent, and social, was the intellectual high ground from which the cult of economic individualism was assailed.

That human nature, like all the rest of nature, is plastic, that neither "fixed forms" nor "final causes" determine its function and career, was Dewey's cardinal belief. He refused to believe that anything in modern science argued otherwise, and thus he stood against the hosts of instinctivists, geneticists, social determinists, and Freudians, who conceived human nature as a limited given. He drew heavily upon Darwin, primarily to demolish the fixed-species concept, never to support a human instinct theory that was also fixed and purposive. The psychology he favored treated mind as body without treating intelligence as inherited, individual, and innate. With all the sociologists, he placed learning in a social matrix; but he insisted, with certain sociologists like Ward, that intelligence can change its mold. In parrying the fatalistic implications of science wherever they obtruded, Dewey was able to assert that men were equal, not because of their original gifts, but because of their limitless capacity for growth. Thus he hit at Sumner's idealization of social inequality without having to take refuge in the insular individualism of natural rights.

The human organism, wrote Dewey, is not passive because it is plastic. "The organism does not stand about, Micawberlike, waiting for something to turn up. It does not wait passive and inert for something to impress itself upon it from without."[2] The medieval view of reason as a reflector of antecedent truths, the associationist view of mind as a catch box of sensations, the behaviorist view of man as the respondent to stimuli—all these neglected the activistic side of behavior. Dewey's psychology was voluntaristic and functional: man's habits are forms of "executive will"; stimuli are things he discovers; ideas are plans for action, true when shown to work. Unlike Freud, Dewey believed that a dynamic psychology made social change inevitable. For it proved that man was not merely an observer of, but an ac-

[2] *Reconstruction in Philosophy* (New York, Holt, 1920, p. 86; Mentor Book edition, pp. 82–83).

tive, purposeful force within, his environment. "There is no such thing in a living creature as mere conformity to conditions. . . . In the interests of the maintenance of life there is transformation of some elements in the surrounding medium. The higher the form of life, the more important is the active reconstruction of the medium."[3] The social reformer, therefore, had merely to redirect ongoing activity, not to overcome inertia—a task far simpler than the Sumners of social theory ever allowed. Yet there was also a warning note in this conception. The reformer must pay close attention to the means he uses. Reform that coerces impulse loses its vast potential support; reform that represses impulse will one day have to reckon with it.

What of the thinking side of man? Traditionalists in education indict Dewey for letting the primitive urges of children set the norms and goals of instruction. Catholic and neo-Thomistic writers accuse him of annihilating reason in a naturalistic—that is, "merely" materialistic—formula. These critics, however, ignored Dewey's clear intentions. It was no Rousseauist who insisted that nurture was as important as nature and that the "constructive use of intelligence" was the prime goal of education. It was no ally of irrationalism who summed up a half-century's faith by writing: ". . . the only alternatives to dependence upon intelligence are either drift or casual improvisation, or the use of coercion. . . ."[4] By naturalizing reason, by making it a more complex, indirect, and reflective mode of organic behavior, Dewey hoped to make it more, not less, effective than it had been before. He broke early with Hegelianism in order to take reason out of its cloister as a spinner of ideal truths and put it to work on concrete problems. The thinking process—

[3] *Ibid.*, p. 85; p. 82.
[4] *Liberalism and Social Action* (New York, Putnam, 1935), p. 51.

the awareness of a doubtful situation, the definition of the problem, the framing of hypotheses, the elaboration of their consequences, the experimental validation or test—was, Dewey believed, as efficacious in day-by-day situations as in the organized pursuits of science. If intelligence thus conceived provided no absolute certainties, no grasp of essences or eternal truths, it yielded warranted, though tentative, assertions—which for Dewey was certainty enough. The eighteenth-century dictum "man is rational" and the nineteenth-century dictum "man is animal" were fused in Dewey's dictum that thought and action, mind and body were one.

For Dewey, these words—plasticity, impulsiveness, intelligence—described human nature only when related to another—sociality. The individual, in order to grow, needs the sympathetic assent of others: "in interactions alone are potentialities realized." A secure emotive life needs "definite social relationships and publicly acknowledged functions." Intelligence "depends upon the methods and conclusions that are a common possession." This was the point where Dewey crossed from psychology into social criticism with the most significant results. Society, he held, does not consist of economic men but of whole personalities; social interaction is not described by the process of purchase and sale but by the communication and sharing of experience; social harmony does not result by awarding cash to individual effort but by wide participation in efforts of common concern. To be sure, the cohesion he desired had to be conscious and voluntary or it would not do. In *Individualism, Old and New* (1930) he attacked the haphazard standardization of life and taste in America which created "corporate and collective results" without the "sense of social fulfillment." And in *Freedom and Culture* (1939) he berated the Russian dictatorship for its solidarities imposed by force.

What Dewey wanted was functional communities and free individuals. He never felt that he sought opposites, reconcilable only in a verbal or metaphysical sense. In what he took to be the holistic and emergent implications of modern science, "social" was not the antonym of "individual" but its fuller description.

With these ideas, Dewey furnished assurance to a progressive generation that individual freedom and social reform were compatible. He became its philosopher-in-chief, its link between the tradition of diversity and the corporate pulls of the twentieth century. But he was not its guide to where difficulty and injustice precisely lay. This was partly due to his viscous prose, but then, Marx inspired social action with scarcely more grace of style. This was partly because Dewey—in his writing though not in his comportment—was more concerned with the syntax of the problem than with its idiom, with its rational rather than its ceremonial forms. Generally speaking, this archfoe of fixed social goals was averse to fixing on definite social targets. It remained for other minds—minds somewhat less subtle and somewhat more concrete—to probe the constitutional, political, and economic practices that perpetuated the inherited cult on the field of action.

All through the nineteenth century, the folk image of a divinely inspired national constitution, checked and balanced so as to render it impartial, made plausible the contention that the state was neutral in economic affairs. It had been in the power of historians to dispel that folk image, to list the property holdings acquired through the connivance of governments, to tell of a constitution born in economic struggle and signifying class victory. But the hand of the genteel tradition had been heavy on the historian's art. The most famous interpreter of the Constitution in the nineteenth century had been George Bancroft, whose doctrine that the Constitution came from Providence and the right reason of the Founding Fathers led to the conclusion, as Max Lerner put it, "that the Almighty must have been a Federalist." In addition, a group of scholars led by Herbert Baxter Adams at Johns Hopkins and John W. Burgess at Columbia studied constitutional history as a product of the genius of the Teutons rather than as a product of the needs of Americans. Meanwhile, as their scholarly works helped to adorn the folk image, American historians came to pay their respects to objectivity, to the Rankean ideal of history "written as it actually happened"—an ideal that merely served to make their prejudgments somewhat less explicit. Indeed, what uses history had for disenchantment had been discovered mostly by nonhistorians. Toward the end of the century, the heretical economist Thorstein Veblen studied economic institutions as barbarian survivals, and, somewhat later, the socialist Gustavus Myers traced the history of great American fortunes back to their source in public franchises and land pre-emptions.

With the publication in 1913 of Beard's *An Economic Interpretation of the Constitution,* a new epoch began for American historical scholarship in general, for thinking about the Constitution in particular, and for the approach of the American mind to the subject of government. Structurally, the book was quite simple. Slowly, almost tediously, but inexorably, Beard moved down three main steps. First, he presented a catalogue of the economic interests represented at the Constitutional Convention, showing that the small farmer and the mechanic had been excluded, and that the large security holder, land owner, banker, and trader had predominated. Second, he analyzed the text of the Constitution to ascertain which interests were abetted by its provisions. The third step drew the conclusions indicated by the other two.

> The Constitution was not created by "the whole people" as the jurists have said; neither was it created by "the states" as Southern nullifiers long contended; but it was the work of a consolidated group whose interests knew no state boundaries and were truly national in their scope. . . .
> The Constitution was essentially an economic document based upon the concept that the fundamental rights of private property are anterior to government and morally beyond the reach of popular majorities. . . .[5]

There had been, to be sure, anticipations of Beard's conclusions in the works of A. M. Simons and J. Allen Smith. But the scholarly efficiency with which Beard marshalled heretofore neglected Treasury documents, the calm effrontery with which he quoted from the Founding Fathers to disprove their presumed neutrality, the bloodless prose in which he draped the provocative thesis of protocapitalism versus democracy—these devices made the book altogether exceptional. Moreover, it was timed exactly for the right season: opposition to big business had reached its climax in the election of 1912 and the elevation of Wilson, while the Supreme Court threatened to wield the Constitution in the trusts' defense. Inevitably, the response to the book was more passionate than perceptive; inevitably, its allegorical value submerged its importance as history. Conservatives like Nicholas Murray Butler were quick to link Beard to the "crude, immoral and unhistorical teaching of Karl Marx," despite Beard's claim that Madison was his model and despite the fact that the historian's roots were Midwest progressive with a touch of Fabian. Political

[5] *An Economic Interpretation of the Constitution* (New York, Macmillan, 1935), pp. 324–25.

progressives, on the other hand, regarded the book as an inexpugnable bit of muckrake and did not perceive that Beard's facts were incomplete (did the men of '87 buy their government securities before or after they wrote the Constitution?), that his analysis was not, and was not meant to be, all-explanatory (did the constitutional provision for civil supremacy arise directly from class interest?), and that his conclusions were at points ambiguous (did he mean to assert the psychological fact that the founders were primarily motivated by gain or the sociological fact that their perspective on good and evil was colored by class associations and values?). Scholarship and life had been joined, but at the expense of the calm assessment scholarship requires.

Beard aimed at something much broader than a political tract of the moment; he intended his analysis of the Constitution to exemplify a general theory of constitutional government. In the form of an incomplete syllogism, this theory was presented in the very first chapter of the book. The major premise was as follows: ". . . the primary objective of government, beyond the mere repression of violence, is the making of rules which determine the property relations of members of society." The conclusion was: ". . . the dominant classes . . . must perforce obtain from the government such rules as are consonant with the larger interests necessary to the continuance of their economic processes, or they must themselves control the organs of government."[6] The minor premise, implied in the above and in a book called *The Economic Basis of Politics* (1922), was that men tend to rationalize their class interests and pursue their class interests rationally. It was a significant revision of classical liberal theory. Large propertied interests had long acted on the covert understanding that the state was a prize, not a referee; Beard made this understanding explicit and used it for lib-

6 *Ibid.*, p. 13.

eral reform. Genuine diversity, he was saying, was not achieved by the mathematics of addition and division—by the formula of "each man, one vote" or by the separation of powers. For it was not abstract equal individuals who counted but economic groups, and the separation of powers was a device for checking majority interests in the legislature. True diversity in politics, therefore, was achieved only when the state registered the pressures of all interests accurately. Beard's pluralism was Dewey's sociality principle, spelled out for political action.

Insofar as Beard accepted the notion that economic motives predominated over others, he did not depart from the determinism of the inherited cult or its narrow psychology. In this respect, the economic interpretation of history and politics was untouched by Dewey's inspiration. But after World War I and the failure of the liberal program, Beard also came to see experience as changing and indeterminate. Disillusioned, he went further than Dewey: under the influence of Croce's idealism and Mannheim's sociology of knowledge, he ended his quest for certainty by making an absolute out of uncertainty. An animated defense of historical relativism, delivered in the form of a presidential address before the American Historical Association in the thirties, demonstrated how far he had traveled from his economic interpretation. Because every event in history is richer in content than the historian's account of it, because the values that determine the selection of material are existentially determined, Beard concluded that the writing of history was never a scientific operation but always an act of faith.[7] He had, indeed, always maintained that he had

7 See Charles A. Beard, "Written History as an Act of Faith," *American Historical Review*, XXXIX (January 1934); also "That Noble Dream," *American Historical Review*, XLI (October 1935).

written "an" interpretation of the Constitution and not "the" interpretation; but now, as a relativist, his position was that he had written an interpretation good for the year 1913. This prepared the ground for his retreat in the mid-forties. Reacting to the spread of fascism, Beard declared that the Founding Fathers had performed a universal service in framing a government of laws not men (*The Republic,* 1943). In a revised edition of *The Economic Basis of Politics* (1945) he took a 180-degree turn and declared that the political man in the modern world overruled the economic man. But—it is often the case with seminal thinkers who live long and change their minds—Beard could not change his earlier impact by applying later qualifications. In a symposium conducted by the *New Republic* in the era of the New Deal, liberal American intellectuals reckoned Beard's work on the Constitution one of the two most influential books in changing their minds.[8] Stronger by Beard, a generation had grown up ready to probe the "symbols of government," "the folklore of capitalism," and the "tyranny of words."

No less than the historian, the nineteenth-century jurisprudent built a breastwork for the cult of economic individualism. Philosophers of the law gave free enterprise metaphysical grounding: in natural rights, in free will, in limited government as a Platonic Idea. Practical corporation lawyers found property safeguards in constitutional texts: in "due process of law"; in the legal "personality" of corporations; in "life, liberty and property"; in "equal protection of the laws." And the judges on state and federal courts—whose backgrounds often included both the practice

[8] *Books That Changed Our Minds,* eds. Malcolm Cowley and Bernard Smith (New York, Doubleday, 1939), pp. 19–20.

of corporation law and an interest in jurisprudence—put regulative legislation through the double gauntlet of philosophical and constitutional review. Public regulation of railroad rates had to conform to the philosophical-common law concept of "reasonableness" or be set aside; public regulation of hours and wages in industry ran afoul of the constitutional term "liberty" (read: "liberty of contract") and rarely survived. Moreover, with their tendency to regard the Constitution as a set of Mosaic rules valid for all time, the judges, like the historians, did not concede their ideological bias. Even as they struck down the income tax law and applied the penalties of the Sherman Act to labor, the Fields, the Fullers, and the Peckhams on the Supreme Court maintained that their decisions were discoveries, not inventions; their organon was logic, not predilection; their judgments were universals, not products of time, place, or class.

While the brethren of the courts were making economic individualism a fixture in immutable law, a colossal figure was working among them and challenging their basic assumptions. Oliver Wendell Holmes, Jr., had become a judge on the Massachusetts Supreme Court in 1882, and had risen to the United States Supreme Court in 1902, where he remained for thirty years. Temperament—not ideology—brought Holmes into conflict with dominant juristic opinion. Attracted to the semantics of pragmatism, Holmes was affronted by the "delusive exactness" with which judges defined property; to Holmes, property was not a "thing" but "a course of action" fraught with consequences. A scholar in revolt against legal scholasticism, Holmes wrote his learned book *The Common Law* partly to show that "the felt necessities of the time" rather than the syllogism determine the rules of men. An artist using law as his medium, Holmes found experience the content of law as art, self-awareness the essence of art as law. But with the passions and compassions of the political progressive Holmes had very little sympathy. This New England aristocrat who had known and admired Emerson, this Civil War officer who considered force the ultima ratio, was not disposed to make the government an eleemosynary institution. Life was, for Holmes, a constant struggle in which more often than not superiority betokened success. Still, the social Darwinist found no friend in Holmes. The strenuousness was there, the conservative economics also, but the cosmic certitude, the urge to represent the familiar as the necessary—these traits were totally lacking. Holmes believed society would not be regenerated by "tinkering with the institution of property"; but he was willing to defer, in a different application of the rule of reason, to a not unreasonable legislator who thought otherwise. An abiding sense of his own fallibility made this conservative the Great Dissenter.

Holmes's viewpoint is most cogently illustrated by his dissent in the *Lochner* v. *New York* case (1905). Judge Peckham, declaring for the court, invalidated a New York State law providing for a ten-hour day in the baking industry. In a sweeping limitation of the state's police power, Peckham held that it abridged the liberty guaranteed by the Fourteenth Amendment. Holmes's dissent projected him into the forefront of liberal jurisprudence, not because it denounced Peckham's politics (it did not), but because it renounced his kind of judicial interference. "This case is decided upon an economic theory which a large part of the country does not entertain. If it were a question whether I agreed with that theory, I should desire to study it further and long before making up my mind. But I do not conceive that to be my duty, because I strongly believe that my agreement or disagreement has nothing to do with the right of a majority to embody their opinions in law." "The Fourteenth Amendment does not enact Mr. Herbert Spencer's *Social Statics*. . . . [A] constitution is not intended to embody a particular economic theory, whether of paternalism and the organic relation of the citizen to the State or of laissez faire. It is made for people of fundamentally differing views, and the accident of our finding certain opinions natural and familiar or novel and even shocking ought not to conclude our judgment on the question whether statutes embodying them conflict with the Constitution of the United States."[9]

Thus the libertarian temper, expressing itself in the doctrine of judicial restraint, opened the door to social experimentation. Did it also open the door to any expedient of the majority, no matter how extreme? Critics of Holmes, particularly the proponents of natural law and ethical absolutism, were convinced that his approach broke down all constitutional safeguards, even those of personal liberty. But the life of a man, to paraphrase Holmes, is not logic but experience. Perhaps inconsistently, Holmes was not willing to exercise, in the area of civil liberty, the restraint he showed in the area of economics. Believing that the Bill of Rights did not embody any absolute guarantees, he nevertheless felt that it provided irreducible minima of freedom. He fought for procedural safeguards in court, for the privacy of the person against legislative and administrative invasion, for freedom of speech except where it presented a clear and present danger to society. In his approach to the diversity-solidarity problem, Holmes permitted a wide gamut of solutions, but there was a point (and there was a point for Dewey, too) where he spoke the absolutist's words: "thus far but no further."

Immediately after the Lochner case, the trend of court decisions seemed to be in line with Holmes's reasoning,

[9] *Lochner v. New York,* 198 U.S. (1905), 45, 74.

but the ebb of the progressive tide and the appointment of conservative judges during the twenties reversed this trend. Year in and year out, Holmes, joined by Justice Brandeis, poured his arguments into that ineffectual void where dissents seemed to go. But vindication, if slow in coming, came unmistakably. The first results were apparent in legal philosophy, where a movement was afoot to change its bias toward economic individualism. Sociological jurisprudence, dedicated to the principle that the law is a social phenomenon to be judged by its fruits in social welfare, rose on a foundation laid in part by Holmes. Its chief proponents, Justice Cardozo and Roscoe Pound, completely rejected the assumption that individual rights antedated positive law or that the maximum assertion of wills had a higher ethical value than the maximum satisfaction of wants. The next step was justification in the courtroom. Following Holmes's dicta on judicial tolerance, the Roosevelt appointees on the Supreme Court validated most of the legislation of the New Deal, including the Minimum Wage and Hour Act. Too late for the great judge to see it, the cult of economic individualism was eventually dislodged from its strongest redoubt.

In the system established by Adam Smith, perfected by Alfred Marshall, and handed on by hosts of nineteenth-century believers, economic activity was pictured as tending toward "normal" goals. Classical and neoclassical economists ranked apprehended facts in terms of their closeness to these preconceived norms, rating those at the farthest remove as "aberrations," "exceptions," or "disturbances." Thus, by assuming that the normal tendency of the economy was to increase production, they regarded depressions as temporary disturbances. By assuming the normal condition of the market to be perfectly competitive, they ascribed the failure of labor, capital, and consumer money to secure their best markets to external causes. The actual operation of economic institutions was obscured and rationalized by the assumption that there was a beneficial propensity—a normal tendency—inherent in economic events.

Peerless in breadth of knowledge, Thorstein Veblen challenged the concept of normality as a qualified philosopher, a student of psychology, a trained and resourceful economist. In an important early article called "Why Is Economics Not an Evolutionary Science," the philosopher of science spoke. The concept of normality—and the kindred notions of an overruling Providence and a moral law of nature—were, to Veblen, carry-overs of a primitive animism. At best, they gave rise to systems of "economic taxonomy," that is, to logically consistent propositions unrelated to life. At worst, they justified a hands-off policy with respect to the price mechanism and the market. Veblen urged economists to adopt a theory of cumulative causation —of emergent evolution—which he felt best explained phenomena objectively as causes and effects.[10] Simultaneously, Veblen exposed the *psychological* fallacies of prevailing economic theory. By conceiving human nature in hedonistic terms, economists normalized men and, by so doing, ignored them. "The hedonistic conception of man," Veblen wrote in his typically ugly but vivid prose, "is that of a lightning calculator of pleasures and pains, who oscillates like a homogeneous globule of desire of happiness under the impulse of stimuli that shift him about the area, but leave him intact."[11] As long as man is a passive and inert thing, he can

[10] "The Preconceptions of Economic Science," *Quarterly Journal of Economics,* XIII (January 1899); (July 1899); XIV (February 1900).

[11] "Why Is Economics Not an Evolutionary Science?", *Ibid.,* XII (July 1898); and reprinted in *The Place of Science in Modern Civilization* (New York, Viking, 1930), p. 73.

be summed up and disposed of by supply-demand schedules. But the human organism is dynamic: it has a "propensity to emulation" and an "instinct of workmanship" which find expression in ways that shape and are shaped by the impinging culture. The proper study of economics must proceed, therefore, from a knowledge of social psychology and the cultural context.

Veblen's interest was not in method for method's own sake. With the publication of *The Theory of the Leisure Class* (1899) and *The Theory of Business Enterprise* (1904) he revealed the enormous implications of this new methodology for social criticism. In the present stage of cultural development, wrote Veblen, the propensity to emulate is satisfied by pecuniary success and dominates the instinct of workmanship, which is fulfilled by productive efficiency. The leisure class and the business enterprise are the institutional forms of this development. Strategically located in industry because of the prerogatives of ownership, businessmen seek pecuniary success by inflating and deflating values, by wrecking and reorganizing business, by sabotaging production, by creating depressions. Occupying a similar strategic place in society, the leisure class seeks pecuniary reputability by abstaining from productive work, by conspicuously consuming and lavishly wasting, by creating a whole complex of futile activities ranging from collegiate sports to religious rituals. Technology, a community product, creates our riches; business, an individualistic enterprise, creates our wastes. Thus, with his malicious taste for paradox, Veblen regarded the very phenomena subordinated or overlooked by economic normalists—depressions, monopolies, all forms of non-serviceable economic actions— as normal in the sense of being typical or characteristic of the present order.

In attacking the roots of inherited economics, Veblen left considerable doubt as to his own roots and connections. He seemed to go beyond progressivism to a solidaristic extreme when he urged at one point that the engineers run the economy for greater efficiency. For a time he was in precarious vogue with American socialists, but he disappointed them, too, when he made it clear that he did not accept, among other things, the dialectical inevitability of socialism. Unable or unwilling to make the decorous adaptations that academic life required, Veblen developed few ties to school or place. It was not surprising, therefore, that when he pictured the modern Jew as a "wanderer in the intellectual no-man's land," many considered this a camouflaged statement of his own detribalized state. But the legend of Veblen as an intellectual nomad, while not altogether inaccurate, tends to neglect the elements in his thought that were of conventional progressive design. His attack on the cult of economic individualism, his belief that social change could be effected only through changes in habits of thought, his opposition to norms disguised as scientific law, and his presentation, withal, of descriptions full of normative judgments—these bear the progressive stamp. Dewey's dynamic psychology (somewhat attenuated by a spurious instinct theory) and Holmes's antipathy to natural law (somewhat strengthened by a knowledge of eighteenth-century metaphysics) are both recognizable in Veblen. In one respect, however, Veblen was unlike the others: he fathered no significant movement in his chosen profession. To be sure, the intelligent lay public took up some of his aphorisms and made them common coin, and makers of public policy after the Great Depression followed his thinking in setting up such controls of business enterprise as the Securities and Exchange Commission. But few professional economists other than Wesley Mitchell and John R. Commons carried on his analysis and method. It was the Englishman Keynes, not Veblen, who was to drive home the antinormalist argument from different premises and reaped the reward of a devoted and influential following.

The almost simultaneous appearance of two great appreciations of education—John Dewey's *Democracy and Education* (1916) and Henry Adams's *The Education of Henry Adams* (1918)—proves that the progressive argument did not sweep the field. Adams considered diversity in most of its forms—differences in belief, democracy in politics, multiformity in culture—as symbols of social degradation. The past and the future met in this conception. The eidolon of an ancestral puritanism was visible in his contention that man, having lost his sense of unity with God, would not find it again with man. The pessimism of Spenglers- and Eliots-to-come was reflected in his doubts —years before Victorian civilities were threatened by revolution and all civilization by total war—that technological advance meant progress. In an era of mostly cheerful prognoses, Adams saw only "the persistently fiendish treatment of man by man; the effort of society to establish law, and the perpetual building of authority against the law it had established; . . . the perpetual victory of the principles of freedom, and their perpetual conversion into principles of power."[12] This was an anachronism and a prophecy.

All through his life Adams endeavored to find the laws of social devolution, as though to know them would be to make his mind a citadel against chaos. Had his training been evangelical, he might have sought a renewal of faith; but the spirit of Jonathan Edwards was extinct in this worldly

12 *The Education of Henry Adams* (Boston, Houghton, 1918), p. 458.

Bostonian. Had his training been psychoanalytical, he might have sought the answer in eruptive drives; but he was too much the eighteenth-century rationalist to truck with the unconscious. Trained to write history, taught to love art, ambitious to apply science, Adams assimilated history to physics, God to symbol, society to force. In his *A Letter to American Teachers of History* (1910) he tried to apply the second law of thermodynamics to history, treating all forms of active energy, organic and inorganic, individual and social, as a "vast clockwork running down." In *Mont-Saint-Michel and Chartres* (1904) and in *The Education* he elaborated another theory—a theory that society was moving in a comet's orbit, which, having reached the thirteenth-century perihelion of unity (as symbolized by love of the Virgin and by the cathedral of Chartres), was accelerating back to an outer darkness of diversity (as symbolized by the impersonal power of the dynamo). No formula truly satisfied him, yet no formula was rejected merely because it was reasoned strictly from analogy.

The universal elements of *The Education* are not to be found in the universal laws proposed toward the end of it but in the broad meanings flowing from intimate experience throughout the book. Writing in the third person, the standoffish Adams had the ability also to stand off from himself. His education represents the quest for values in a world that stresses technique; his isolation, the fixed price the intellectual must pay in a thoroughly acquisitive society. Yet the detached mood of this autobiography does not quite conceal the personal reasons for his uniquely somber philosophy. His cynicism poorly covers his pride in a family that produced two presidents of the United States and one famous diplomat-statesman, that looked on high public office as a legacy and acquitted it as though it were a trust. His self-depreciation hardly hides his ambition for power and his disappointment when the politics and politicians of Grant's era denied that ambition. There is a strong suggestion that Adams was first repelled by the Medusa face of American society—its hostility to tradition and receptivity to novelty, its indifference to intellect and submission to wealth—when it turned this face toward him and his aspirations. Between Dewey's world-not-yet-made and Henry Adams's world-running-down lay interstellar space, and this was the distance also between their respective chances for leadership.

The progressive required a context of peace. With the country at war in 1917–18 he lost his bearings and succumbed, under the excitation of war and Wilsonian rhetoric, to that mixture of martial symbols and apocalyptic hopes with which America goes to battle. "Every month which the war continues," wrote John Dewey, prophet of gradual reconstruction, brings "an awakened sense for human affairs," a "psychological and educational advance."[13] "In such a vast crisis as war," again wrote John Dewey, advocate of the disciplined intelligence, "there is something wholesome in the popular feeling which regards absence of indignation, and an excessive exhibition of balanced judgment, as signs of apathy as to the ends of war."[14] It was the opinion of Charles A. Beard, iconoclastic historian, that "victory for the German imperial government would plunge all of us into the black night of military barbarism."[15] "When a nation is at war," wrote Oliver Wendell Holmes, cutting

[13] "The New Social Science," *The New Republic*, XIV (April 6, 1918).

[14] "The Cult of Irrationality," *The New Republic*, XVII (November 9, 1918).

[15] "Letter of Resignation from Columbia University," *School and Society*, VI (October 13, 1917).

the edges of the First Amendment and his own libertarian principles, "many things that might be said in time of peace are such a hindrance to its effort that their utterance will not be endured as long as men fight and that no court could regard them as protected by any constitutional right."[16] Only Thorstein Veblen, though he privately supported the war, retained his usual enigmatic pose: his *Imperial Germany and the Industrial Revolution* (1915) was both banned from the mails under the Espionage Act and accepted as propaganda by the Creel Committee on Information.

History records their violent disillusionment and recoil. Even before the Armistice, Dewey had forebodings of disaster; after Wilson failed at Versailles, his repentance was complete. In *The New Republic,* a journal which had done most to spur progressives to the Great Crusade, Dewey confessed that "we took to war our sentimentalism" and "a policy of suppression of free speech . . . and of violent unrestraint characteristic of the reactionary."[17] Holmes, as though to atone for his failure to protect Eugene V. Debs with the "clear and present danger" criterion, wrote a ringing defense of intellectual freedom in the Abrams case. "[W]hen men have realized that time has upset many fighting faiths, they may come to believe even more than they believe the very foundation of their own conduct that the ultimate good desired is better reached by free trade in ideas —that the best test of truth is the power of thought to get itself accepted in the competition of the market."[18]

But it is always easier to go to Canossa than to be received there. Many supposed that if progressives had been led into error, progressivism was deficient in truth. Was the common man's desire for freedom, as progressives believed, resolute

---

16 *Schenck* v. *United States,* 249 U.S. (1919), 47.

17 "The Discrediting of Idealism," *The New Republic,* XX (October 8, 1919).

18 *Abrams* v. *United States,* 250 U. S. (1919), 624.

and general, lacking only rational articulation to social norms? The experience of the war argued otherwise. The ritual of the loyalty oath, the persecution of pacifists and other deviants, the flowering of superpatriotism, and the use of reverential national symbols revealed the still potent tribal instincts of coercion and taboo. Randolph Bourne, whose *Youth and Life* (1913) and *Education and Living* (1917) had sung Dewey's praises, turned apostate when the progressives and the country went to war. "A philosopher," he wrote, referring to John Dewey, "who senses so little the sinister forces of war ... who assumes that the war-technique can be used without trailing with it the mob-fanaticisms, the injustices and hatreds that are organically bound up with it, is speaking to another element of the younger generation than that to which I belong."[19] According to Bourne, the very philosophy of progressivism contributed to this grave misjudgment. The progressive had relied naïvely on the common man's intelligence and had underestimated the craving for security. Without fixed goals for a people in crisis, he had encouraged blind, doubt-resolving action. He had become swallowed up by the masses and had let "great incalculable forces" bear him on, all in the fantasy of leadership. Bourne's was but a cry of despair, heightened by a sense of betrayal; but it heralded the war generation emerging from the holocaust to find, in F. Scott Fitzgerald's words, "all Gods dead, all wars fought, all faiths in man shaken."

iii—Rotarian Bombast and Social Negation

The solidarist mood bred in war persisted, in different forms, throughout the ensuing decade. The intolerance of the war patriot had its afterimage in the Legionnaire and

---

[19] "Twilight of Idols" in *Untimely Papers* (New York, B. W. Huebsch, 1919), pp. 115–16.

the Ku Klux Klansman. The officiousness of the war censor was kept alive by the fundamentalist saving the young from Darwin, and the prohibitionist saving everyone from the fermented grape. The further rationalization of capitalist enterprise in this period fed this solidarist spirit. The mass production of merchandise required the standardization of tastes and a last overpowering assault on that display of individuality called consumer resistance. In an otherwise mechanized economy, salesmanship remained a prized and special skill; next to the public school, the advertising agency became the foremost adversary of individual and cultural differences.

For business leaders and apologists, the pure cult of economic individualism, useful as ideology while capital was being amassed in oil and steel, was less useful when inventories were heaped in radios and cars. Sales promotion in a depersonalized society was not to be served by iterating the gospel of ruthless competition, even when this was coupled with the promise of ultimate harmony. Thomas Nixon Carver, the Harvard economist, led the Ivy Lees and the Bruce Bartons in revising the business credo with more directly solidaristic concepts. Carver depicted an economic revolution in the United States which, he declared, was making the "struggle philosophy" of Spencer and Sumner obsolete. In the new age, he submitted, laborers were investing in business and adopting the viewpoint of capitalists; producers were reducing costs and coming over to the viewpoint of consumers. The old-time patriarchal interest of the businessman in his community was reappearing under the rubric of Service; that mutuality of interest characteristic of a simpler economy was being revived by profit-sharing. What was particularly attractive about this new order was that it maintained the institution of private property and the incentive of private profits. Under the leadership of business, particularly of big business, America was finding, wrote Carver, that it can have "freedom from authority combined with freedom from poverty and . . . need not choose between the two."[20] Carver soldered economic individualism to social solidarity in the heat of the Golden Glow.

But to a small and brilliant minority, all that American society offered in the twenties was a catchpenny opportunism in economics and regimentation in everything else. They found true diversity blighted in the land, and each reacted to this state of affairs as he defined diversity or understood the causes of blight. To some, like Malcolm Cowley, Matthew Josephson, and Harold Stearns, the fault lay in the entire American culture: the uniformities and banalities of the Jazz Age were but the late fruits of puritan and pioneer values. For them the only way left to defend diversity—vaguely defined as the right of the individual to be erratic, erotic, or esoteric—was to become liberated from conventionality, and so they filled the Bohemias of the cities or sought total insulation in exile. For others, like H. L. Mencken, the fault lay in the torpidity of the "herd mind," and diversity—construed as the right to debunk dogma—was a privilege the superior mind had always to wrest from the unwilling group. Still others, of whom Walter Lippmann was an important example, located the ailment in the complexities of the Great Society and saw the problem of protecting diversity as part of the larger problem of applying independent judgment to a world of indirect experiences.

All of these critics were enmeshed in the same paradox:

20 *The Present Economic Revolution in the United States* (Boston, Little, 1925), p. 46.

in the name of a waning diversity, they attacked the democratic order in which only it grows. Confronting the fact that
most Americans submitted willingly to "normalcy," they
leaped to the *non sequitur* that majority rule was the cause.
Facing the universal centralizing tendencies of capitalism,
the standardizing pressures of a consumer-oriented economy, the weakening of inherited moralities, they based their
analysis on narrow political grounds or on invidious aesthetic objections. Having no faith in the progressive synthesis,
their reply to solidarity by Rotarian bombast was diversity by social negation. The tragedy of their position was
that they attacked democracy for being unified around banalities and indirectly gave aid to those forces which were
unifying men still more thoroughly around the mysticism of
race and war.

Harold Stearns, editing an obituary of American culture
on behalf of the Lost Generation, merely proved that what
that generation lost was historical perspective. To him and
to most of the thirty-three intellectuals contributing to *Civilization in the United States* (1922), Billy Sunday and Roger
Williams, Warren Harding and Thomas Jefferson were all
of a single piece: "We have no heritage or traditions to
which to cling except those that have already withered in
our hands and turned to dust." Finding in the whole of
America and her complex history only "emotional and aesthetic starvation," only a "mania for petty regulation,"
Stearns wanted nothing less than "an entirely new deck of
cards."[21] Whereupon he embarked for Europe, a continent
about to demonstrate the lengths to which the mania for
regulation could go.

Mencken's indictment of democracy stemmed from a set
of prejudices that mixed mysticism with science—the Nie-

21 *Civilization in the United States* (New York, Harcourt, 1922), p. viii.

tzschean transvaluation of values with the conclusions of the
Simon-Binet test. With a vast resource of invective and sar-
casm, Mencken indefatigably documented what he called
the "war of democracy on civilization." Democracy attempts
to iron out its superior men, "to pump them dry of respect,
to make docile John Does out of them. The measure of its
success is the extent to which such men are brought down
and made common. The measure of civilization is the extent to which they resist and survive."[22] The politics of
democracy churns mediocrities and hypocrites to the top.
"The demagogue is one who preaches doctrines he knows
to be untrue to men he knows to be idiots. The demaslave
is one who listens to what these idiots have to say and then
pretends to believe it himself. Every man who seeks elective
office under democracy has to be one or the other, and most
men have been both."[23] As far as proposed remedies were
concerned, the attack on the demos had not improved in its
passage from Henry Adams to H. L. Mencken. With a sweep
of pen, Mencken dismissed progressives and socialists as par-
tisans of the Christian "slave morality"; they were, like all
reformers, levelers, meddlers, men without style or humor.
If anything could be done about democracy it would have
to be done through eugenics; but biological planning offered at best slow relief—"it takes as much time to breed a
libertarian as it takes to breed a race horse"—and Mencken
looked forward to a long open season on Bryan-baiting and
Babbitt-hunting. Somehow it did not occur to him that
there was a positive correlation between the great popularity of his books and the tolerance, and even possibly the
sophistication, of the republic. Nor did it occur to him that,
by his reckoning, two generations of Baltimore Menckens

[22] *Notes on Democracy* (New York, Knopf, 1926), p. 151.
[23] *Ibid.*, p. 103.

were hardly enough to produce himself, archlibertarian that he was, unless the environment had benignly intervened. Nor did the season last as long as he surmised: this insolent commentator of the twenties, who was also its vibrant representative voice, became tiresome and unpopular when economic disaster overtook the country and constructive answers were needed.

Walter Lippmann was a more complex case. Here was a disillusioned progressive in whom the seriousness and high purpose of progressivism had not died. If Stearns represented an elite too tender for the frictions of American life, Lippmann hoped for an elite that would stop "drift" with intellectual "mastery." If Mencken was content to poke fun at *vox populi*, Lippmann studied the dynamics of public opinion. And yet, because it was more responsible than the usual critique of democracy in this period, and because it garnered the deeper insights of Sigmund Freud, Robert Michels, and Graham Wallas, Lippmann's argument rendered the more telling blows.

The belief that the average man was competent to know and judge all public issues was what Lippmann called the "mystic fallacy of democracy." The first clue to political wisdom, he thought, was in knowing that there intervenes between man and social reality a pseudo environment, a world-as-imagined, which is a counterfeit and a distortion of the world-as-is. To find his place in the "blooming, buzzing confusion," the average man utilizes stereotypes, ideas that are more comforting because they are definite than discomforting because they are wrong. Experience cannot validate nor reason correct these stereotypes, for the experience of the average man is local, partial, and impoverished, and reason provides no cure for faulty premises. The consequence is that the average mind is prey to propagandists, machine bosses, and pressure groups: to all the makers and purveyors of stock ideas for special purposes. This, then, is the crux of the problem: democracy calls on the average man to decide the "oughts" without giving him a chance to know the "facts."

In the traditional correctives for this situation Lippmann put no stock. The appeal to education, he felt, was barren, for the world changes faster than the teacher's lesson plans. The appeal to the referendum and the direct primary was not more fruitful: it rested on the illusion that the average person would have a "better public opinion because he is asked to express his opinion more often." Nor would socialism in any way alleviate this problem; it would exaggerate it rather, by creating "an enormous complication of political interests that are already much too complicated."[24] All of these nostrums supported the fallacy—operative since the days of Jackson—that "the compounding of individual ignorances in masses of people can produce a continuous directing force in public affairs."[25] To Lippmann, the correct approach had to lie in the opposite direction: in compounding expert opinion and in minimizing the influence of sheer numbers. He proposed that a corps of social scientists be constituted to ascertain facts and clarify goals—to separate, in short, appearances from social realities. He urged that the general public be allowed only to decide the validity of general rules, that the normal functions of the legislator pass to fact finders and administrators. Lippmann's prescription for democracy's illness—as old as Plato's remedy—was a continuing dose of *expertise*.

Perhaps no one but an "automatic" democrat would contest Lippmann's belief that public opinion in a democracy

[24] *The Phantom Public* (New York, Harcourt, 1925), pp. 37–38.
[25] *Ibid.*, p. 39.

is often unstable, credulous, and unenlightened. On the other hand, only the exponent of sheer efficiency as the highest public good would accept his solution. Grant, however, that the purpose of a democracy is to provide a prophylaxis against the abuse of power, and then public opinion becomes all-important—not in disposing issues but in deposing men. Grant that social stability is a desideratum, and then the public's assent to laws becomes the only alternative to compelled obedience or revolutionary resistance. Grant, moreover, that the growth of the citizen in political maturity, however slow, is a socially important goal, and then no purpose can be served in having him think and vote entirely by proxy. Oddly enough, as witness *The Good Society* (1937), Lippmann did grant these propositions, maintaining that the loss of the freedom to err, at least in economic matters, might be more dangerous than the errors themselves. But this was in reaction to Roosevelt's criteria of efficiency and the New Deal type of expert—and hence it reflected an even greater distrust of public opinion and its mandates.

iv—The Social Engineer and the Ideologues of Left and Right

A long deluge of depression dispelled the social atmosphere of the twenties, washing away most of its creeds and obsessions. Much to the discredit of the patriarchal business ideology, the Pecora Investigation revealed that respected Wall Street banks had mulcted their patrons, and the Brookings Institution proved that production lagged behind capacity even in the bonanza days. The war of the intellectuals against democracy was stilled: Nazism loomed as a greater threat to culture; the idle machine was more terrible than the machine triumphant; in a time of trouble, the market was good for themes that affirmed "the people, yes." The social questions Americans now asked were elemental and practical: how can we find security? how can we stop totalitarianism? The more thoughtful put these questions together: how much and what kind of economic planning is compatible with political and personal freedoms? Many Americans, in this period, thought the problem of reconciling diversity and solidarity was like the problem of building a bridge: that is, it had to be actively attacked, experimentally tested, expertly directed, with allowances for stresses and strains.

Not so, however, the doctrinaires on the extreme left or right, for whom the word "planning" mobilized dogma, and the word "freedom", general propositions. For example, orthodox Marxists, whom Lewis Corey then represented in their Leninist-Stalinist form, decreed that anything short of the overthrow of capitalist relations was not "planning" but retrogressive "state capitalism." With real insight, Corey pointed out that freedom was contracted and made hollow when there was mass unemployment, that a choice was not meaningful when it was a choice to eat or to starve. From this point in actuality, Corey went on to a purely conventional analysis. By definition, capitalism, because of its internal contradictions, tends toward the concentration of ownership, the pauperization of the masses, ever deepening depressions. Therefore, capitalism must become the enemy of the liberty it once had fostered and must turn, at a certain stage in crisis, to outright repression of liberty—to fascism. Only the dictatorship of the proletariat could avert this reactionary climax. That the medicine would not be as disastrous as the disease was dialectically assured: "Where capitalism starts with the ideal of 'limited government' and ends with the all-devouring 'totalitarian' state of fascism, socialism starts with the dictatorship of the proletariat and ends with the dissolution of the state into the community of integrally organized producers."[26] This proposition—out of dictatorial order, freedom—put as much strain on belief as the reverse magic of the nineteenth-century cult—out of autonomous action, order. More influential than its few outright and enrolled believers would indicate, Marxism never had the influence that conservatives feared. Roosevelt proved to the masses of Americans that partial reform could be efficacious, and the Moscow trials belied the freeing effect claimed for revolutionary potions.

No more than the Marxists did the neoliberals on the right seek out the degrees, limits, and measurements of the planning problem. Walter Lippmann started from an important truth in *The Good Society:* every plan endangers the freedom of individuals because it must decide fundamental questions of value, and it must do so over a long period of time. Again the argument deteriorated into logic. If to the Marxists economic planning, to be effective, had to be total, to Lippman economic planning tended to be total whenever it was effective. "[T]he search for security and a rational society, if it seeks salvation through political authority, ends in the most irrational form of government imaginable—in the dictatorship of casual oligarchs, who have no hereditary title, no constitutional origin or responsibility, who cannot be replaced except by violence."[27] The quietism Sumner achieved by speaking for a pitiless cosmos was achieved by Lippmann speaking for the limited imagination.

[26] *The Decline of American Capitalism* (New York, Covici, Friede, 1934), p. 539.
[27] *An Inquiry into the Principles of the Good Society* (New York, Little, 1937), p. 105.

David Lilienthal refused to be guided by the futilitarians of the left or of the right. "My purpose is to show by authentic experience in one American region," wrote the director of the Tennessee Valley Authority, "that to get such new jobs and factories and fertile farms our choice need not be between extremes of 'right' and 'left,' between overcentralized Big-government and a do-nothing policy, between 'private enterprise' and 'socialism,' between an arrogant red-tape-ridden bureaucracy and domination of a few private monopolies."[28] What did it require to find the golden mean? First, the juxtaposition of two kinds of knowledge: knowledge of technology and science, and knowledge of democracy and morals. Second, the preservation of two kinds of faiths: that "there is nothing, however fantastic, that (given competent organization) a team of engineers, scientists and administrators cannot do today"; and that "tested principles of democracy" provide "a philosophy and a set of working tools (which) can guide and sustain us in increasing opportunity for individual freedom. . . ."[29]

To Lilienthal, solidarity did not have to be superimposed by edict; it was present in nature's own unities. The Tennessee River winding through seven states was unity, the valley of the Tennessee was unity, the region embracing the valley was unity. The efficiency and wholeness of view desired by the solidarist could be achieved by attacking the interlocking problems of these entities: by curbing the river's flood, by landscaping the artificial lakes, by conserving the flora and fauna, by improving transportation, by producing and selling electric power cheaply to the valley's people. Moreover, there was no need to barter freedom for kilowatt-hours. In the principle of decentralization—by

[28] *TVA; Democracy on the March* (New York, Harper, 1944), p. xi.
[29] *Ibid.*, pp. xi, 3.

which TVA became free in its detailed operations from the center at Washington—and in the principle of grass-roots democracy—by which local societies, co-operatives, councils, demonstration farms were brought into voluntary co-operation with the experts—Lilienthal thought he discovered a way to keep democracy on the march, to reconcile the power of machines with the needs of personality.

Many of the most significant motifs of the half century blended in Lilienthal's lyrical book. Here was the spirit of science, less promiscuous than its nineteenth-century kin, but not a bit less buoyant. Here was the crisp competence of the administrator: the concern with quantities and degrees, the indifference to the logic of either/or. Here was social theory offered as a postlogue of action—a rarity in the chronicles of social thought. And here was the broad humanism of the progressive—a faith in the capacity and goodness of ordinary men when freed from circumstantial blight, a concern with men as ends not means. Now, at the century's mid-point, when nations are paying devotion to utility and force, this last trait seems almost archaic. But it is certain that only when it exists in strong measure is there a possibility that diversity and solidarity can be effectively conciliated.

A Selected Bibliography

I. PHILOSOPHY IN AMERICA

Adams, G. P., and W. P. Montague, (eds.). *Contemporary American Philosophy: Personal Statements.* New York, The Macmillan Company, 1930. 2 vols. Consists of philosophic autobiographies by a large number of American philosophers, covering every shade of opinion.

Bergmann, Gustav. "Logical Positivism" and "Semantics" in *A History of Philosophical Systems,* ed. V. Ferm. New York, Philosophical Library Inc., 1950.

———. "A Positivistic Metaphysics of Consciousness," *Mind,* LIV n.s. (July 1945), 193–226.

———. "Psychoanalysis and Experimental Psychology: A Review from the Standpoint of Scientific Empiricism," *Mind,* LII n.s. (April 1943), 122–40; reprinted in *Psychological Theory,* ed. by M. H. Marx. New York, The Macmillan Company, 1951.

Black, Max. "The Linguistic Method in Philosophy" in his *Language and Philosophy: Studies in Method.* Ithaca, Cornell University Press, 1949.

Farber, Marvin, (ed.). *Philosophic Thought in France and the United States.* Buffalo, N. Y., University of Buffalo Publications in Philosophy, 1950. One half of this book is made up of essays representing contemporary American trends.

Feigl, Herbert. "Logical Empiricism" in *Twentieth Century Philosophy,* ed. D. D. Runes. New York, Philosophical Library Inc., 1943.

———, and W. Sellars. *Readings in Philosophical Analysis.* New York, Appleton-Century-Crofts, Inc., 1949.

Hook, Sidney, (ed.). *John Dewey: Philosopher of Science and Freedom* (a symposium). New York, Dial Press Inc., 1950.

Krikorian, Y. H., (ed.). *Naturalism and the Human Spirit.* New York, Columbia University Press, 1944. A collection of essays presenting "naturalistic" approaches to various problems of philosophy.

Montague, William P. "The Story of American Realism" in *Twentieth Century Philosophy,* ed. by D. D. Runes. New York, Philosophical Library Inc., 1943.

Perry, R. B. *The Thought and Character of William James.* Cambridge, Harvard University Press, 1948. An indispensable intellectual and cultural history, this work contains a full bibliography and the letters of James to his family, friends, and colleagues.

Royce, Josiah. *The Philosophy of Loyalty.* New York, The Macmillan Company, 1908. Concrete application to ethics: "loyalty to loyalty."

———. *The Spirit of Modern Philosophy.* Boston, Houghton Mifflin Co., 1892. The nonhistorical sections of this book contain the most readable expositions of Royce's philosophy.

Schilpp, Paul Arthur, (ed.). *Library of Living Philosophers.* Evanston and Chicago, Northwestern University Press. These volumes, a unique and most important contribution to philosophic discussion, consist of interpretative and critical articles by various writers on famous living philosophers, together with the philosopher's reply to his critics. Complete bibliographies of Dewey, Santayana, and Whitehead can be found in the volumes below.

——, *The Philosophy of John Dewey*. Evanston and Chicago, Northwestern University Press, 1939.

——, *The Philosophy of George Santayana*. Evanston and Chicago, Northwestern University Press, 1940.

——, *The Philosophy of Alfred North Whitehead*. Evanston and Chicago, Northwestern University Press, 1941.

Sellars, Wilfrid, and John Hospers. *Readings in Ethical Theory*. New York, Appleton-Century-Crofts, Inc., 1952. Contains the most important recent literature in the field, American and British.

Weinberg, Julius Rudolph. *An Examination of Logical Positivism*. New York, Harcourt, Brace and Company, 1936; London, Kegan Paul, Trench & Trubner, Ltd., 1936. Exposition and critique.

II. The Journalist as Literary Man

Beach, Joseph W. *The Outlook for American Prose*. Chicago, University of Chicago Press, 1926.

Conklin, Groff, (ed.). *The New Republic Anthology: 1915–1935*. New York, Dodge Publishing Co., 1936.

Kramer, Dale. *Ross and the New Yorker*. Garden City, N. Y. Doubleday and Company, Inc., 1951.

Millett, Fred B. *Contemporary American Authors*. New York, Harcourt Brace and Company, 1944.

Morris, Lloyd. *Postscript to Yesterday: America, the Last Fifty Years*. New York, Random House, Inc., 1947.

Spiller, Robert E., *et al.* (eds.). *Literary History of the United States*. Vol. III. New York, The Macmillan Company, 1948.

Sullivan, Mark. *Our Times: The United States*. New York, Charles Scribner's Sons, 1926–36. 6 vols.

III. American Social Thought

Beard, Charles A. and Mary R. *America in Midpassage* (Vol. III of *The Rise of American Civilization*). New York, The Macmillan Company, 1939.

Commager, Henry Steele. *The American Mind: An Interpretation of American Thought and Character Since the 1880's*. New Haven, Yale University Press, 1950.

Curti, Merle. *The Growth of American Thought*. Second Edition. New York, Harper and Brothers, 1951.

Gabriel, Ralph Henry. *The Course of American Democratic Thought: An Intellectual History Since 1815*. New York, Ronald Press Company, 1940.

Kazin, Alfred. *On Native Grounds, An Interpretation of Modern American Prose Literature*. New York, Reynal & Hitchcock, 1942.

Madison, Charles A. *Critics and Crusaders: A Century of American Protest*. New York, Henry Holt and Company, 1947.

Spiller, Robert E., *et al.* (eds.). *Literary History of The United States*. Vols. II and III. New York, The Macmillan Company, 1948.

White, Morton G. *Social Thought in America: The Revolt Against Formalism*. New York, Viking Press, 1949.

INDEX

INDEX